DRUGS
101

DRUGS 101

101

AN OVERVIEW FOR TEENS

MARGARET O. HYDE AND
JOHN F. SETARO, M.D.

TFCB TWENTY-FIRST CENTURY BOOKS
MINNEAPOLIS

Names of patients and cases have been modified to protect privacy.

Text copyright © 2003 Margaret O. Hyde

Photographs courtesy of Photo Researchers, Inc: pp. 10 (© A. Dex/Publiphoto), 27 (© Richard Hutchings), 75 (© James Prince), 128 (© George B. Jones III); Corbis Sygma: pp. 18 (© Neri Grazia), 39 (© Houston Scott); AP/Wide World Photos: pp. 53, 101; Woodfin Camp & Associates: p. 65 (© Chuck Nacke); Getty Images: p. 81 (© Michael Smith/Newsmakers); PhotoEdit: pp. 85 (© David Young-Wolff), 95 (© Mary Kate Denny), 109 (© Amy Etra); Magnum Photos: p. 105 (© Ferdinando Scianna); Gamma Press USA, Inc.: p. 114 (© Brooks Kraft)

Twenty-First Century Books
A division of Lerner Publishing Group
241 First Avenue North
Minneapolis, MN 55401 USA

Website address: www.lernerbooks.com

Library of Congress Cataloging-in-Publication Data

Hyde, Margaret O. (Margaret Oldroyd), 1917–
    Drugs 101 : an overview for teens / Margaret O. Hyde and John F. Setaro.
      v. cm.
    Includes bibliographical references and index.
    Contents: Drugs: the changing scene—Addiction and the brain—Marijuana, heroin, cocaine, and methamphetamine—Club drugs—Prescription drugs and inhalants—Drugs and the young brain—Drug abuses, you, and society—Starting and stopping: prevention and treatment—Reducing the supply—Should drugs be legalized?
     ISBN-13: 978-0-7613-2608-3 (lib. bdg. : alk. paper)
     ISBN-10: 0-7613-2608-1 (lib. bdg. : alk. paper)
     1. Teenagers—Drug use—United States—Juvenile literature. 2. Drugs—United States—Physiological effect—Juvenile literature. 3. Drug abuse—United States—Prevention—Juvenile literature. [1. Drugs. 2. Drug abuse.]
I. Setaro, John F. II. Title.
HV5824.Y68 H975 2003
362.29'0835—dc21   2002008290

Manufactured in the United States of America
3 4 5 6 7 8 – BP – 10 09 08 07 06 05

CONTENTS

DRUGS 101

I thought you had to be a heroin or cocaine user to be a drug addict. Or at least you had to be thirty years old. I tried E (ecstasy) because my boyfriend said it was good stuff. He didn't tell me it was so good I would not be able to stop taking it. Now, they say I'm psychologically addicted to it, whatever that means.

An ecstasy user

CHAPTER 1

DRUGS:
THE CHANGING SCENE

WHAT ARE DRUGS?

Drugs can make you feel wonderful or terrible; they can do many things. There are beneficial drugs that can be used to help heal the body, make it feel better, and keep it well. There are also many drugs that are abused, some that have medicinal purposes and others that have no medicinal uses whatsoever.

Drugs that are abused are chemicals that are expected to cause changes in mood or ability, such as alcohol, nicotine, marijuana, heroin, and cocaine. Except for alcohol and nicotine, which are legal for adults, most of these mind- or mood-altering drugs are illegal. The downside of nicotine and alcohol has been well publicized and is well understood. The truth about other drugs that affect the mind is more difficult to find.

Not everyone who tries drugs has the same experience. Not everyone who uses drugs abuses them. Some young people experiment with drugs and stop, but some slip quickly from being users to abusers without realizing this is

A teenage boy snorts cocaine.

happening. They become addicted and can't stop. No one knows which users will become quickly addicted.

WHY DO PEOPLE USE DRUGS?

The drugs people abuse fall into six or seven basic categories: cannabinoids, depressants, dissociative drugs, hallucinogens, narcotics, stimulants, and other compounds such as anabolic steroids and inhalants. The kind of intoxicating effect a drug produces plays a part in the user's choice.

Some drugs, such as the *cannabinoids*, hashish and marijuana, and the *narcotics* heroin and opium, produce euphoria and relieve pain. *Depressants*, such as alcohol, flunitrazepam, and GHB, can reduce pain and anxiety, lower inhibitions, and produce feelings of well-being. *Dissociative drugs* such as ketamine and PCPs, distort perceptions of reality, while *stimulants,* such as amphetamines

10

and cocaine, can increase alertness, relieve fatigue, and produce feelings of exhilaration and strength. *Hallucinogens*—ecstasy, LSD, and the like—alter perceptions and feeling.

WHO ABUSES DRUGS?

Even though most people do not abuse drugs, it sometimes seems that they do. Drugs are part of the life of a ten year old who inhales paint thinner and an elderly man who takes sleeping pills each night. They are part of the life of the binge-drinking college student, the pot-smoking kid in the bathroom of a rural school, and the stately congressman who belts Scotch after Scotch while telling his friends he is sponsoring a law that will keep kids off drugs. Timothy Leary, Harvard professor and cult leader, succeeded in wrongly persuading many teens of the 1960s that LSD not only was harmless but also the door to an exciting experience.

About 16 million people in the United States abuse drugs, according to National Families in Action (NFIA) 2002 figures. More than one in ten young people aged twelve to seventeen used drugs. Year after year, teens report that drugs are the most important problem they face.[1]

THE CHANGING SCENE

Drug use and abuse are not new phenomena. People have probably been using and abusing drugs since the beginning of recorded history. Opium was used by the ancient Sumerians and Egyptians. The ancient Scythians, a pastoral nomadic group in central Asia, used marijuana. Indigenous people of the Andean highlands chewed the leaves of the coca plant, the plant from which cocaine is derived, to endure work at high altitudes and low temperatures. Some indigenous people of North America chewed peyote, a stimulant derived from a kind of cactus. The chewing of tobacco is an old custom. European explorers to the New

World carried tobacco back across the Atlantic where smoking quickly caught on.

Drug use has been recorded in mythology, folklore, and literature for centuries. Drugs play a central role in sedating Sleeping Beauty and Snow White. Sherlock Holmes, Sir Arthur Conan Doyle's famous sleuth, used cocaine. Sigmund Freud, father of psychiatry, also used cocaine. He prescribed cocaine as a replacement drug to a friend who was addicted to morphine. After he saw his friend suffering from cocaine addiction, Freud realized that he had been wrong. He stopped his own use of cocaine and other drugs for the rest of his life.

The popularity of some drugs has changed through the centuries. Would you believe it if someone told you that your great-grandmother used paregoric, a weak form of opium, to soothe her crying baby? In the nineteenth century, opium, cocaine, heroin, and morphine were found in many medicines and tonics that could be bought in drugstores. One popular product was "Mrs. Winslow's Soothing Syrup." It contained an opium-based drug and was advertised as having a calming effect on children. Many people became addicted to the drugs in patent medicines without being aware of the fact. Such "medicines" were so plentiful that some call the nineteenth century the dope-fiends' paradise.

Cocaine was popular, and legal, until the 1880s, but after reports were publicized that users often died suddenly from heart attacks and strokes, cocaine was banned in the United States and its use was nearly eliminated by 1920. Cocaine use was revived in the 1980s, when the smokable form of the drug appeared. *Crack*, small chips of purified cocaine, was cheap, very addictive, and very destructive. By 1990 the use of cocaine had dropped again both because of new laws prohibiting its use and because people became aware of the violence and tragedy associated with it. Many violent crimes were committed to obtain crack, and families were neglected by those who used it. Today, crack is spurned by most young people. Children and younger siblings of "crack heads" have seen what the drug did to their relatives, and they turn away from it. In some cases young people have reclaimed whole neighborhoods from drug dealers. But some crack is still around.

For most of the twentieth century, heroin was used mostly by people in inner cities. By the 1990s it was thought of as "yesterday's drug" since its use declined, but today heroin is as common in some neighborhoods as Starbucks.[2] In 2000 the U.S. Department of Health and Human Services reported an alarming rise in the use of heroin by high-school seniors—the highest levels among high-school seniors since the survey began more than twenty years ago.[3]

The use of *ecstasy*, a designer drug that became popular around 1998, continues to increase in use, but the amount of the increase slowed in 2001.[4] A *designer drug* is one that is made in an illicit laboratory to imitate certain controlled substances and circumvent the drug-scheduling law. The growing use of ecstasy, a manufactured version of amphetamine, may be comparable to the rise of crack cocaine in the 1980s, but rather than being sold mainly in inner cities, ecstasy sellers are predominately suburban high-school males who mistakenly think of it as a safe drug. Ecstasy doubled in popularity among twelfth graders from 1998 to 2000. Between 1999 and 2001, ecstasy use by teens increased by 71 percent.[5] Even though the rate of increase has leveled off, it is still popular on the black market.

Illegal drug use began to decrease in the late 1970s, and alcohol consumption in the early 1980s.[6] However, illegal drug use increased among young people between 1990 and

TYPES OF DRUGS USED IN A ONE MONTH PERIOD BY ILLICIT DRUG USERS AGED 12 AND OLDER: 2000

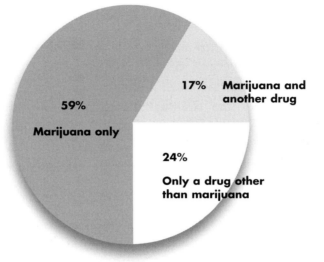

59%

Marijuana only

17% **Marijuana and another drug**

24%

Only a drug other than marijuana

1996.[7] And this was followed by a decrease. A national study, released by the Partnership for a Drug-Free America, indicated that fewer teenagers in America were smoking marijuana in 2000, following a three-year decline.[8]

Although some drugs like ecstasy and OxyContin, a prescription painkiller, are increasing in popularity, this is not the case for most drugs. Recent surveys show that teens in America are turning to drugs less frequently and are finding illicit drug use less acceptable.[9] Since 1998 drug use by most youths has decreased or stayed the same. One exception is steroids. They are used by some teens to build up muscles and improve their sports performance or to achieve a fashionable lean but muscular look. Steroid use is actually on the increase.

SOME CHANGES IN DRUG LAWS

Illegal drug use continues, and laws about drug use continue to change. In 1970, Congress passed the Comprehensive Drug Abuse Prevention and Control Act that established a system of classifying drugs in Schedules I to V, in most cases according to their potential for abuse. The Drug Enforcement Administration (DEA) administers the law.

While marijuana is a Schedule I drug along with heroin and other drugs that are subject to the most severe punishment, laws regarding its use are changing in many places. In some states laws about marijuana use are becoming stricter, and in others they are easing. The possession of small amounts of marijuana has been decriminalized in some states, and a policy of conditional release has been adopted in many more. Conditional release usually lets a first-time offender opt for probation rather than a trial. In some states marijuana has been legalized for medical use. When marijuana is *decriminalized*, it makes the penalties for the private use of small amounts about as serious as a traffic ticket and subject to a fine. Decriminalization is different from *legalization*; growing and selling marijuana are still criminal offenses in all of the United States.

A Gallup Poll in the year 2000 showed that 62 percent of Americans do not favor the legalization of marijuana.[10] Many people believe that decriminalization is a slippery slope that will increase the use of marijuana.

LOOKING FOR ANSWERS

Most young people who have used drugs began using them because a friend or relative persuaded them to try drugs. They may have been looking for a high or a new way to perceive things. Others may be using drugs to escape from depression or to ease the pain of a cruel world. Some may be rebelling against strict rules at home or at school; others may be satisfying their curiosity. But most teens are just looking for honest answers to questions about drugs.

New tools have emerged that help scientists understand how drugs affect brain chemicals and how abuse begins. These techniques are helping to answer questions such as why it is more difficult for some people to stop smoking than for others, why a crack-using mother puts her own drug craving before her baby's welfare, and what happens when teens use marijuana or other drugs for fun.

The estimated 16 million users of illicit drugs affect you and the rest of the population. For those who become addicts, the harm to society is so great that people often say that the nation is awash in illegal drugs. Even though most people do not use illegal drugs and most users are not abusers, drugs are responsible for much crime, poverty, child abuse, lack of health care, failure in school, poor employment history, and a host of other problems. Even limited illegal drug use can harm the young brain. Information about illicit drugs is the main concern of this book.

CHAPTER 2

ADDICTION AND THE BRAIN

Fifteen-year-old Dillon goes online every morning and, using capital letters, he screams his message to the world: "I'M GOING TO QUIT. NO COCAINE TODAY FOR ME." Every day he promises himself he will quit, but he never does. Cocaine has activated circuits in his brain that produce feelings of pleasure and reward. He craves this feeling and uses cocaine again and again. If he doesn't use it, he will suffer severe *withdrawal*. He will sleep for a day or two to restore his energy, and when he awakens, he will decide never to use cocaine again. Two weeks later the craving will start to build. He feels no pleasure in anything, and the craving reaches fever pitch. He will buy and use more cocaine. He is hooked.

WHAT IS ADDICTION?

There are numerous definitions of *addiction*, and addiction can differ with different drugs, but dependence on the drug is always present. A drug is addicting if it causes compulsive, uncontrollable craving, seeking, and use, even in the face of harmful health and/or social consequences.

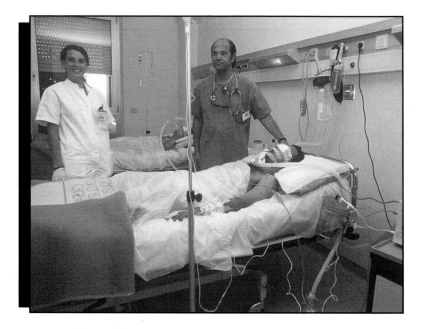

Heroin addicts often must be hospitalized to endure withdrawal treatment.

According to some definitions, addiction has both a physical and a psychological component: The body is dependent on the drug (physical addiction), and the person craves the drug to the point that it becomes a central role in life (psychological addiction).[1]

FROM USE TO ABUSE TO ADDICTION

Which of these statements do you believe is true?

"Drug abuse is a choice."

"Addicts have a brain disorder."

Although these statements are often considered controversial, both are true. In the beginning people choose to use a drug, but once they become addicted, little choice is involved, for they have developed a brain disorder that compels them to seek and take the drug to which they are addicted.[2]

Drug abuse is a complex, dynamic process that affects the brain's structure and functions. If you are an addict, you have taken a "head trip" from which it is very difficult to return. While drugs affect your whole body, the most important effects are in your brain where your brain's natural chemicals are changed by drug use and craving keeps you using drugs again and again. It is much easier to get hooked than unhooked. The English poet John Dryden said, "We first make our habits, and then our habits make us."

DRUGS AND THE BRAIN

Your brain is unbelievably intricate with so many units that it cannot imagine itself. About 100 billion nerve cells, called neurons, occupy the 3-pound (1,362-gram) mass in your head that looks somewhat like soft pudding. These tiny neurons are unique cells that have specialized branches, one of which may connect to thousands or even tens of thousands of other neurons. Hundreds of millions of neurons send messages to one another in a vast communication system in your brain.[3]

Sometimes the brain is compared with a telephone system, but this is not really accurate because there are microscopic gaps in the system that carries the messages in your brain. A gap in a telephone wire or an electric wire would break the circuit. In your brain, messages travel across the gaps, called synapses, by way of special chemicals that move from one cell to another. These chemical messengers are called *neurotransmitters*, and there are about a hundred different kinds of them. Each kind has its own shape and fits into receptors much as a key fits into a lock. Drugs, too, are chemicals, and they can fit into some of the locks made for certain natural neurotransmitters. Drugs move through the blood, and some nestle into the receptors that are used by natural neurotransmitters. The receptors get used to having the illicit drug there instead of the natural chemical, so sometimes they will no longer accept the natural chemical.

Drugs can change the way you feel by changing the way neurons communicate. They masquerade as neurotransmitters in one of two ways: They act as false messengers or they change the strength of real neurotransmitters, changing the way the brain works. There are many systems involved in transmitting messages, and they are highly complex.

In recent years scientists have been able to learn quite a bit about what is happening inside the brain of an addict. With new imaging techniques scientists can actually look at the dynamic changes in the brain that occur when an individual experiences the "rush," the "high," and even the craving for a drug. They can show how addictive drugs take over, or hijack, the brain's reward system and flood the brain with massive amounts of chemicals, especially the neurotransmitter *dopamine*.

Dopamine levels rise in the brain when you pet a dog, hug a friend, eat a chocolate bar, and have any pleasurable experience. When addicts take drugs, ten or more times the normal amount of dopamine is produced. It is this increase in dopamine that scientists have come to believe is characteristic of all addictions.[4] Other characteristics of each drug create different effects on the body. For instance, cocaine speeds up the heart and can cause a heart attack, while heroin slows the respiratory rate by affecting the brain stem and spinal cord.

BECOMING AN ADDICT

Not everyone who uses even very addictive drugs becomes an addict. Only 14 percent of the soldiers who used heroin in Vietnam continued to use the drug when they returned to the United States, even though heroin is a highly addictive

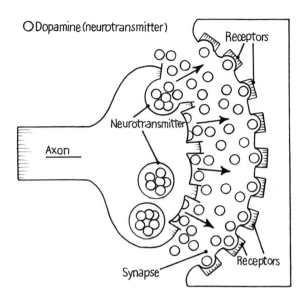

O Dopamine (neurotransmitter)

Receptors

Neurotransmitter

Axon

Synapse

Receptors

Methamphetamine produces pleasurable feelings by increasing the level of the neurotransmitter dopamine at the synapse. Meth gets inside the axons of neurons that contain dopamine and releases dopamine directly into the synapse. This alteration in transmission at the synapse activates the brain reward system.

narcotic.[5] Patients who are given morphine (the drug from which heroin is produced) to relieve pain seldom become addicted to it.

Many young people who experiment with drugs stop before they become addicted. Others become addicted very quickly. Fifteen-year-old Samantha became an alcoholic with her first drink. She is one of a relatively few people to whom immediate addiction happens, but it can happen. Some users get hooked the first time they snort, smoke, or inject methamphetamine, a highly addictive stimulant also known as speed.[6]

Who becomes addicted depends on genetics, body chemistry, environment, and many other factors. About half the risk of addiction may be genetic.[7] A psychological problem may lead to addiction. Low self-esteem, the feeling of being ostracized, and the need for instant gratification seem to be possible springboards to addiction. Unfortunately, there is no way of knowing who will become an addict. Some drugs have stronger addictive properties than others. When rated according to dependence (how difficult it is for the user to quit), nicotine rates highest. After that come heroin, cocaine, alcohol, caffeine, and marijuana. As mentioned earlier, addiction depends on many factors. Most people can drink small amounts of alcohol without becoming addicted to it, but the percentage of smokers who become addicted to nicotine is about 80 percent.[8]

In the United States, about 12 million people are addicted to alcohol, about 50 million to nicotine, about 2 million to cocaine, and 1 million to heroin.[9] If a paper were to advertise for participants in a clinical study of drug addicts, many people would not know whether or not they qualified. Addiction is a disease of denial. This is true no matter what the drug.

THE ADDICTIVE QUALITIES OF POPULAR DRUGS COMPARED
(Higher score indicates more serious effect)

Drug	Dependence	Withdrawal	Tolerance	Reinforcement	Intoxication
Nicotine	6	4	5	3	2
Heroin	5	5	6	5	5
Cocaine	4	3	3	6	4
Alcohol	3	6	4	4	6
Caffeine	2	2	2	1	1
Marijuana	1	1	1	2	3

Source: www.drugwarfacts.org

DEPENDENCE, TOLERANCE, AND WITHDRAWAL

Most people who are addicted to a drug began using it casually for pleasurable feelings or as a way to drown sorrows. Every addict starts out as a casual user. After people are addicted, they use the drug to prevent the unpleasant feelings of withdrawal. The drug has changed their brains so that they feel they must have it, and for many of them, it is the only thing that gives them pleasure. Addicts need the drug to feel normal, so they crave the drug, even if it no longer gives them pleasure. Long-term, repeated use of a drug changes the brain, so the user cannot control drug-taking behavior. The ability to make choices about the use of the drug is impaired because of these changes.

Tolerance develops when drug use is repeated fairly frequently. At first, a small amount of a drug may produce a high, but as the drug use continues, the neurons in the brain adapt to it so larger amounts of the drug are needed to produce the same high. This tolerance happens because the brain becomes more efficient at disposing of the drug and because the cells of the brain change themselves to become more resistant to its effects.

Withdrawal refers to symptoms that come with sudden discontinuation of a drug to which the body has become accustomed. Withdrawal can be mild, as in the case of the coffee drinker who develops headaches because she spends a weekend at a friend's where only decaffeinated coffee is served. A heroin addict's withdrawal is agonizing, and an alcoholic's can be life threatening. During withdrawal an addict's brain must adjust to being without the drug that it has adapted to over a long period of time. When it no longer gets the drug, it has to change the way it functions.

EACH ADDICT IS DIFFERENT

Schuyler has tried a number of different drugs, but he never used them more than a few times. He has not become addicted, and like the great majority of people, he probably never will. However, the first bottle of beer, the first line of coke (cocaine), the first hit of weed launches some individuals on a self-destructive path from abuse to addiction. They have what used to be called an addictive personality. No one knows which people will be vulnerable.

Corbin is very critical of anyone who smokes pot or uses other drugs. He only drinks beer, so he thinks he is not using drugs, but of course he is. He needs his beer to feel normal and to prevent feelings of withdrawal. He is an *alcoholic*, an addict who is unaware of his problem.

No one wants to become an addict, but millions do. In some ways, each addict is different, but all begin by choosing to use a drug in the first place.

Do You Have a Problem with Marijuana?

1. Has smoking pot stopped being fun?
2. Do you ever get high alone?
3. Is it hard for you to imagine a life without marijuana?
4. Do you find that your friends are determined by your marijuana use?
5. Do you smoke marijuana to avoid dealing with your problems?
6. Do you smoke pot to cope with your feelings?
7. Does your marijuana use let you live in a privately defined world?
8. Have you ever failed to keep promises you made about cutting down or controlling your dope smoking?
9. Has your use of marijuana caused problems with memory, concentration, or motivation?
10. When your stash is nearly empty, do you feel anxious or worried about how to get more?
11. Do you plan your life around your marijuana use?
12. Have friends or relatives ever complained that your pot smoking is damaging your relationship with them?

If you answered yes to any of the above questions, you may have a problem with marijuana.

The Twelve Questions are reprinted with the permission of Marijuana Anonymous World Services, Inc. (M.A.) Permission to reprint the Twelve Questions does not mean that M.A. has reviewed or approved the contents of this publication, nor that M.A. agrees with the views expressed herein.

CHAPTER 3

MARIJUANA, HEROIN, COCAINE, AND METHAMPHETAMINE

People become addicted to the popular drugs: marijuana, heroin, cocaine, and methamphetamine in different ways and for different reasons.

MARIJUANA (Pot, Grass, Weed, MJ, Joint, Reefer)

Sixteen-year-old Zach smokes *marijuana*, a cannabinoid that is addictive for about 10 to 14 percent of the people who try it. He has read that marijuana, which is produced from the leaves and flowering tops of the hemp plant (*Cannabis sativa*), is harmful to children and teens, but he has been smoking since he was thirteen and is sure nothing has happened to him. Even though marijuana has at least four times as many toxins and cancer-causing chemicals as cigarettes, he is not worried because he figures he doesn't smoke as often as some tobacco smokers. Besides, scientists can't say for sure what the long-term effects of using marijuana are.

Zach smokes marijuana before school each morning, sneaks off at lunchtime for a joint, then finishes the day

A teen boy smokes grass in his school bathroom.

stoned. But Zach doesn't think he is addicted, even though he is stoned most of the time and marijuana has taken over his life. Like most addicts, he denies his addiction.

One of the important aspects of addiction is the loss of control—the using of a drug despite its negative consequences. Zach spends much of his time under the influence of marijuana, so he has little time to think clearly about what is happening to his grades, to any friends other than the ones he smokes with, to his health, or to his future. His life centers around his drug use. Zach may be one of the people who becomes strongly dependent on marijuana.

> **HASHISH**
>
> Hashish, another cannabinoid, is made from the leaves and stalks of the hemp plant. Its intoxicating effects and potential health consequences are similar to those of marijuana. It is usually chewed or smoked, but is not as popular in the United States as marijuana.

Could Zach stop smoking if he wanted to? It probably would be very difficult. Is he likely to move from marijuana to other more powerful drugs? Maybe and maybe not. For some users marijuana is a *gateway drug*, one that leads to the use of other drugs. Marijuana and other mind-altering drugs increase the amount of dopamine in the brain. Experiments with rats have shown that marijuana interacts directly or indirectly with heroin receptors in the brain as well as with the receptors that are specific for it. This suggests that marijuana may prime the brain for harder drugs. Frequent use of marijuana appears to be a risk factor for heroin use.[1] Alcohol and nicotine, too, are considered gateway drugs. Although most people who use these drugs do so for recreation and do not proceed to heroin or other drugs, most users of heroin have probably used tobacco and/or marijuana first.

Health Effects When most people smoke marijuana, they experience a calm, mildly euphoric effect in which time seems to slow down, music sounds better, social inhibitions are decreased, and taste and smell are enhanced. In addition, short-term memory is reduced and the heart rate increases. Ideas flow rapidly, and the smoker may feel high or hilarious. As with other drugs, dopamine is involved. Delta-9-tetrahydrocannabinol (commonly known as THC), the main active ingredient in marijuana, increases dopamine in the user's system through a complex series of events.

Most marijuana users also experience abnormal hunger. They are famous for going on eating binges they call the munchies. Scientists believe chemicals in marijuana such as leptin reduce the effect of a hormone that tells your body that it is no longer hungry.

The long-term health consequences of using marijuana are still being debated, and scientists admit that they may not all be known for another twenty years. They do agree that it is particularly harmful to children and teens.

Some heavy marijuana users develop tolerance to the drug and in time must increase the frequency and amount they smoke to achieve the desired euphoria, but there are questions about whether or not heavy smokers suffer withdrawal. Scientists have been able to produce mild withdrawal symptoms by using a chemical that prevents delta-9-THC from binding to receptors in the brains of heavy users, indicating that it is present. But, normally, the slow rate at which marijuana leaves the body prevents any obvious withdrawal.

Whether or not longtime users develop dependence, more than 120,000 people per year enter treatment for their marijuana addiction, and Marijuana Anonymous World Services has numerous chapters around the world. The slow rate at which marijuana leaves the body has serious consequences. Marijuana continues to affect the ability of users to pilot a plane, drive a car, operate machinery safely, or make emergency decisions long after the high has passed.[2]

HEROIN (Junk, Dope, Horse, H)

Alexis, who smoked marijuana with Zach every night, wanted some real adventure. She was curious about heroin. Some people warned her not to try it because she might get hooked. But she was sure she could stop using marijuana whenever she wanted, so why worry about heroin? She had read that some people use heroin without getting addicted, and she decided she could be one of them.

The whole ritual of using heroin excited Alexis. After a friend prepared the drug and injected it in her arm, she felt a rush—a rolling wave of euphoria followed by a feeling of being detached from the world. She felt happy and listless. She didn't care that she could not remember anything; all her pains and cares had floated away. Then she went "on the nod," an alternately drowsy and wakeful state.

When Alexis awoke, she was introduced to a group of people who were addicted to heroin. She listened to them talking about their habit and learned how much time they had to spend each day getting enough money for a fix. Some of them spent each day stealing from stores, begging from friends and strangers, or working at jobs that paid just enough to cover their food and their heroin.

Alexis heard these stories but felt they had no application to her. She couldn't imagine that she would get hooked on heroin, yet she became an addict after only a few fixes. For a while she was one of the heroin addicts who manages to hold jobs that pay them enough to keep them in the supply they need for a short period of time. But since tolerance develops, she constantly needed more and more heroin. Fortunately, she never hit rock bottom. Before she ran out of money and suffered other problems common among heroin addicts, she was lucky in being admitted to a treatment center. There she was given *methadone*, a narcotic often administered daily by clinics to addicts to reduce their cravings for heroin and wean them off of it.

Health Effects *Heroin* is a highly addictive opiate that is produced from morphine. Like all opiates, it enters the brain rapidly. Just a few hits and you can be hooked for life. Opiates and opiate receptors are present in the brain and many other parts of the body, and it is possible that heroin and other opiates substitute themselves for the natural drugs. Through a complex process, they release increased amounts of dopamine, and this acts directly on certain neurons in the brain to produce powerful feelings of pleasure.[3]

Heroin is commonly called junk, perhaps because that's what some users say it has done to their lives. Heroin can cause nausea, confusion, and constipation and often leads to serious health and other problems. Most heroin addicts develop health problems because they no longer care for their health properly. Many acquire HIV/AIDS, hepatitis, and other diseases from sharing dirty needles.

Many heroin addicts experience periods of sedation and unconsciousness, and some die from overdoses caused by using impure drugs or drugs that are more pure and therefore stronger than usual. Most heroin is cut with sugar, starch, or powdered milk before being sold. Typically, it is 40 percent pure, but some batches can be as high as 90 percent pure. Users can never be sure what they are taking, so they are always in danger of overdosing.

Researchers at the UCLA Drug Abuse Research Center, who studied 581 male heroin users over a period of thirty-three years, found that the men in the group died earlier than average, suffered from the risk of hepatitis, sexually transmitted diseases, including HIV/AIDS, and had criminal justice problems. The most common cause of death was an overdose.[4] Many addicts are arrested for drug possession, stealing, or selling drugs to get money for their own supply. "In the life" is an expression some use to describe their addiction. No one thinks they mean a happy life.

COCAINE AND CRACK
(Coke, C, Candy, Charlie, Flake, Rock, Snow, Toot)

Zach's friend Marley smoked marijuana with him on weekends but wanted to experiment with other drugs. One Saturday night she got some cocaine and thought it was really cool. Zach suggested that she leave cocaine alone because he had heard how addictive it was, but Marley was sure she would not become addicted to it. She thought of addicts as people with needles stuck in their arms, and her plan was to just sniff a little cocaine once in a while.

But Marley found cocaine to be "out of this world," and she couldn't limit herself to once in a while. She started spending weekends with a gang who snorted cocaine all the time. Because the drug was expensive, she began stealing money from the cash register at work to pay for it.

Within a month, Marley realized things were getting out of hand, and she vowed to go back to smoking pot. But the time never came when Marley gave up cocaine. She just couldn't stop. Cocaine made her feel alert, energetic, and self-confident, even powerful. She felt like a superhero until the cocaine wore off and she crashed. Then she wanted more. She didn't understand that the cocaine was changing her brain, and even if she had understood this, she wouldn't have cared. The high was worth anything.

32

Marley eventually switched from snorting coke to smoking crack, because it was cheaper and more available. Crack gave her a high twice as fast as cocaine, but the crash that followed was even worse. Each crash was characterized by intense feelings of depression, agitation, and fatigue. More crack seemed like the only way to feel good again. Marley's life continued to spiral downward, and eventually she landed in jail.

Health Effects *Cocaine*, a drug made from the leaves of the coca plant, increases the amount of dopamine in the brain. Normally, the dopamine that crosses synapses is pumped back to the neurons that released it after it has delivered its message. Cocaine blocks the pump, called a dopamine transporter, and dopamine then builds up in the synapses between neurons. As a result the dopamine keeps affecting the nerve cells after it should have stopped. This produces the high that cocaine users seek.

Cocaine is also a powerful stimulant—one of the most powerful found in nature.[5] It constricts the blood vessels, making the heart beat harder to pump blood through the body. When this happens, the heart beats faster and can lose its natural rhythm, a condition that sometimes ends in a stroke or heart attack. Even first-time cocaine users can experience seizures or fatal heart attacks.

Cocaine is extremely addictive. Scientists have found that a single use of cocaine can modify nerve connections in the brain, and this may help explain how easily occasional drug use can progress into a compulsion. Experiments with mice at the University of California at San Francisco showed that a single exposure to cocaine usurped a mechanism in the cells that is involved in the normal learning process. Such changes may be important in the early stages of addiction. They may also help to explain how a single exposure to cocaine after a period of abstinence can induce renewed drug-seeking behavior.[6]

METHAMPHETAMINE
(Crank, Speed, Meth, Chalk)

Dan was a senior in high school whose unfinished science paper was due in two days when he first used speed. Although Dan seldom used drugs, he felt that he needed extra energy to stay up for the forty-eight hours he needed to finish his paper. A friend suggested that he get some meth (*methamphetamine*), a powerful stimulant, so that he could make his deadline.

"Everyone does it," usually didn't cut it with Dan, but this was an emergency. He bought some meth in gelatin capsules, gulped one down with water, and went to work on his paper. In a short time, Dan was full of energy. The drug stimulated his reward/pleasure center and signaled his brain that hunger had been satisfied. The drug kept him working for about six hours, then he felt depressed, so he repeated the dose. Dan worked for two days, turned in the paper, and then crashed. He slept for a day and a half.

Although Dan thought his paper was excellent, his grade was not good. Disturbed thinking is typical of meth users. When they are high, they feel powerful and consider their work excellent. When they come down, they find that what they have done is inferior to what they might have done under normal circumstances. But Dan liked the powerful way meth made him feel, and he began snorting meth regularly on weekends with his friends. Although he knew that he could get AIDS from sharing needles with people, sometimes he injected meth anyway. He found that by injecting meth, it got to the brain really fast. Right after injecting speed, Dan felt an incredible rush, an intense sensation that some people compare with sexual feelings. His heart pounded and his skin sweated, and when the rush passed he would experience about five hours of high energy.

In time, Dan developed a tolerance to meth, so he needed larger quantities to produce a rush. He tried taking pills by mouth and snorting it. Although these methods produced euphoria, they did not give him the rush he was looking for. He explored the smokable form of meth (called ice, crystal, glass, or ice cream) without knowing that it is even more addictive than crack.

When Dan reached the point of needing meth every day, he sought help from his parents, who entered him in a rehabilitation program. There he suffered withdrawal, characterized by drug craving, depressed mood, disturbed sleep patterns, and increased appetite. Unfortunately, there are no ideal drugs available to treat addiction to or overdoses of meth. Some agents, such as beta-blockers, calcium blockers, and valium can help limit problems, but counseling and support are the usual treatment.

Health Effects Meth is an *amphetamine*, a drug that stimulates. In the brain, meth can block the re-uptake of dopamine by the neurons that originally release it. Normally, dopamine is removed from the synapses by a chemical pump. This pump rapidly ferries dopamine out of the synapse and deposits it back into the ends of the nerve cells where it is either destroyed or recycled. Meth blocks the pump, so more dopamine is trapped in the synapse where it restimulates the dopamine receptors and produces a powerful high. Meth also increases the level of dopamine by getting inside the nerve terminals and releasing dopamine directly into the synapse. This makes it a potent activator of the reward system. So what is wrong with that?

Although dopamine is a good thing in the amounts found naturally in the brain, too much can mean trouble. When the rush passes, the heart stops pounding and the sweating subsides, but the user is left with a high state of energy. Some users go on binges, or "runs," that last from three to ten days by ingesting meth again and again. During this time they have excess energy, so they don't eat or sleep. To use up energy, one user cleaned his apartment over and over, dumping out the contents of the vacuum cleaner and vacuuming it back again. Users may dance for days, take a car apart, paint the house, clean the floors with a tooth-brush, or use excess energy in any way they can. The run puts a strain on the heart and nervous system and is fol-lowed by extreme depression and lethargy. Side effects of the extended state of euphoria can range from mild panic to *hallucinations* (imagined experiences that seem real) and extreme paranoia. Some users become violent. Prolonged use can result in suicidal or homicidal thoughts.[7]

All kinds of amphetamines speed up the way the body works. They make the heart work faster, and they pump adrenaline into the system. Methamphetamine abuse can damage small blood vessels in the brain, produce inflam-mation of the lining of the heart, and cause a stroke. Chronic meth users exhibit symptoms that can include anx-iety, violent behavior, confusion, and insomnia. Chronic abuse can lead to psychotic behavior in which there is intense paranoia and visual and auditory hallucinations. In heavy users, too much dopamine can even induce schizo-phrenia in a normal person, producing hallucinations and paranoia that are symptoms of this disease. In most cases the symptoms stop when the drug use stops. Researchers have reported that prolonged exposure to low levels of amphetamine can damage as much as 50 percent of the dopamine cells in the brain.[8] Long-term users sometimes feel that bugs are crawling over their skin. The effects of meth, or speed, can be so devastating that the slogan "speed kills" developed as far back as the hippie years.

ADDICTION CAN BE TREATED

For many teens, the intense pleasure they get from drugs is worth the risk of using to the point of addiction if they do not know how hard it is to quit. Except for those who die from an overdose or are poisoned by the impurities in a drug, there is hope of making the long and difficult trip back from addiction through treatment. But there is no cure. Just as most alcoholics cannot take just one drink, other addicts cannot return to their drugs without problems.

CHAPTER 4

CLUB DRUGS

You can go to a rave, trance, club, or other party without taking *club drugs*, but chances are you will see them used there. *MDMA* (ecstasy), ketamine, *GHB, Rohypnol*, methamphetamine, and *LSD* are some of the club drugs gaining in popularity. A club drug is a party drug, one typically used at raves. Most club drugs are hallucinogens or dissociative drugs.

MDMA— 3,4-MethyleneDioxyMethamphetamine (Ecstasy, E, Hug Drug, XTC, Love Doves, Love Drug, M&Ms, Biscuits, Rhapsody, Adam)

Ecstasy, as its name implies, can produce feelings of well-being, peacefulness, and exhilaration. It can reduce inhibitions and make you feel more sensual. It can give you energy and reduce pain to the extent that you can dance all night. It is one of the drugs of choice at raves,[1] all-night parties where large groups of people ride into another world armed with lights, lasers, and the booming bass of music. They dance for hours on end, and in many cases, they share drugs. Individual beliefs are brought together in one throbbing community. Peace, Love, Unity, and Respect (PLUR)

This young ecstasy user carries a pacifier to relieve jaw clench-ing, a common side effect of ecstasy use.

are the four pillars of the rave scene, feelings often experi-enced after taking club drugs. Ecstasy has found its way into mainstream society, so you may come across it at parties and other social events.

Health Effects Ecstasy is classed as a chemically modi-fied amphetamine that has psychedelic as well as stimulant properties. It is similar in structure to methamphetamine, or speed, and causes the brain to release more *serotonin*, one of the chemicals that carry messages between nerve cells and is critical to normal experiences of mood, emotion, pain, and a wide variety of behaviors.

Ecstasy is a stimulant that can increase the heart rate, blood pressure, and metabolism. It is its stimulative effects that enable users to dance for as much as a few days. But, like most drugs, ecstasy has its downside. Undesirable effects can include hallucinations, feelings of loss of control, anxiety, panic, loss of reality, irritability, and depression.

Ecstasy can cause jaw clenching and teeth grinding (for which users sometimes suck on lollipops or pacifiers for relief), chills, double vision, and sweating. Ecstasy-using dancers who chew gum and dance all night may develop sore jaws and badly bruised or blistered feet that may not be noticed until the next day—after the pain-dulling quality of ecstasy wears off. In high doses, ecstasy can cause a marked increase in body temperature leading to muscle breakdown with heart and kidney failure that result in death. It can cause reduced appetite, weight loss, hyperthermia, and impaired memory and learning. Since it destroys serotonin neurons, it may make users more violent. Because the drug seems to mask the sense of thirst, it may also lead to dehydration. Some ravers dance all night and all day until dehydration makes them pass out on the dance floor. Ecstasy users have died of acute dehydration.[2]

Ecstasy's full effects last from three to six hours, but after the released serotonin has been used, there may be a hangover that some users call "Blue Monday." Depression, sleep problems, confusion, anxiety, and paranoia have been reported even weeks after the use of ecstasy. For many, an ecstasy "Blue Monday" is not as bad as an alcohol hangover, but there may be long-term effects.

Dr. George Ricaurte, who studies club drugs at the Johns Hopkins Bayview Medical Center asks, "Have these people put themselves at risk for neurological problems?"[3] Dr. Ricaurte has done extensive research on the effects of ecstasy with brain imaging. He found that memory and the ability to think are affected in heavy users, where long-term use appears to cause permanent brain damage. Many researchers believe that even relatively small doses over a period of months may cause long-term effects on memory and the ability to reason.[4] Scientists say that it is not clear that any dose is safe.[5] There is concern that damage from ecstasy may not appear for years after use.

Ecstasy is made in illegal labs, yet many ecstasy pills are marked with common logos such as Mitsubishi, VW, Rolls Royce, and Nike to make users feel that they are safe. But these companies have nothing to do with the drug, and there is no standardization of dosage. Ecstasy is supposed to contain pure MDMA, but a user never knows what is in a street drug. A dose may be fine one time and kill you the next. Dr. Edward Krenzelok, director of the Pittsburgh Poison Center at Children's Hospital, suggests that taking a rave drug is like finding an open bottle with liquid on the side of the street, picking it up, and drinking from it.

Briana had the time of her life dancing after taking one ecstasy pill, but Jonah, whose ecstasy was laced with a toxic substance, passed out. Pills sold as ecstasy have been found to contain a number of different drugs, especially PMA (para-methoxyamphetamine). This drug can seem like weak ecstasy because it takes about a half hour longer than ecstasy to take effect. Then it produces a mild euphoria, a stimulant effect, and minor hallucinations. PMA can lead to convulsions and coma. When users take PMA thinking they have taken weak ecstasy and ingest another pill to get a better high, the result may be an overdose and death.[6] Ecstasy is cheap to make, but PMA is even cheaper. Other drugs, such as speed and DXM, a cheap cough suppressant that is dangerous in high doses, have been found in ecstasy pills as well.

At one time it was thought that ecstasy was not addictive, but now many users say they are hooked on the emotional high that it gives. They cannot give it up no matter how terrible they feel afterward. Tolerance appears to develop with frequent use. Then it takes two pills to experience the effect of one pill. Dayna Moore, who began using ecstasy at age fourteen, spoke at a hearing on July 30, 2001, before the Senate Government Affairs Committee when she was sixteen years old.[7] "I was a normal kid, and ecstasy took me down a deadly destructive path that I could never have imagined. I spent years chasing the first magical high and that chase nearly killed me."[8] Dayna tried a number of drugs including cocaine after her introduction to ecstasy and spent time in a residential treatment clinic.

KETAMINE
(K, Special K, Vitamin K, Cat Valium, Bump, Honey Oil, Special la Coke; Ketajet, Ketalar are registered trade names)

Ketamine is an anesthetic that makes the user feel as if the mind is separated from the body. It was developed in 1962 to replace the animal anesthetic PCP (phencyclidine or angel dust), and it has become popular as a club drug. Most of the ketamine that is sold illegally for human use is stolen from veterinarians. Although ketamine is manufactured for veterinarians as an injectable liquid, for club use it is usually evaporated to form a powder that can be snorted or compressed into pills.

Nineteen-year-old Sarah's first experience with ketamine was a very bad one. She went to a rave hoping that she would get in with the cool kids, even though she never liked parties. At this all-night party, with thumping music and elaborate light shows, a boy who was high offered Sarah some white powder with the promise that it would make her feel wonderful for forty-five minutes. He said it was special K and that lots of kids used it at raves. Sarah looked at her watch and decided she had two hours before it was time to leave, so she snorted the white powder. Within seconds her lungs stopped working and her body convulsed. She stopped breathing for eight minutes before the ambulance came, and during this time, her brain was without oxygen. The paramedics used electric shock to get her heart working again and rushed her to a hospital. When she eventually came out of her coma, she was paralyzed and her brain was severely damaged. Despite many hours in rehab, where she had to be taught again to crawl and do other things that toddlers do, she will never be able to care for herself. Sarah had snorted a heavy dose of ketamine. Since it is not a regulated drug, no one knows how strong a supply is.

Joyce's first experience with ketamine was also tragic. Ketamine is one of several *date-rape drugs*—odorless, colorless drugs that predatory boys sometimes slip into the drinks of girls so they can rape them. Other drugs used as date-rape drugs are GHB and Rohypnol.

Joyce went to a party with some of her friends where they met some boys from another school. When Joyce wasn't looking, one of the boys slipped some ketamine into her drink. Joyce passed out and the boy raped her. When she woke up a few hours later, she had no recollection of what had happened or how she got there. She felt that someone had had sex with her, but she didn't remember anything about the incident.

Health Effects Ketamine is a dissociative anesthetic—it distorts perception of sight and sound and creates a feeling

43

Reducing the Risk of Date Rape

- Don't accept drinks from an open container.
- Don't share or exchange drinks.
- Be aware of the color, texture, and taste of your drinks.
- Don't leave your drinks unattended.
- Don't accept beverages from someone you do not know well or trust.
- Don't drink from a punch bowl.
- When at a bar or club, accept drinks only from a bartender, waiter, or waitress.
- Carry money for a phone call or taxi.
- Be careful not to let alcohol or other drugs decrease your decision-making ability.

If you suspect that you have been raped, call 911 and ask for help from a rape crisis center. Tests can be made to determine if a date-rape drug is present in your body and whether semen is in your vagina.

of being separated from one's physical body. Ketamine acts by altering the distribution of the chemical glutamate that is involved in the perception of pain, memory, and responses to the environment.[9] Since ketamine is an anesthetic, it is not surprising that users stop feeling pain. After ten to twenty minutes, they may find themselves hardly able to move, and at higher doses, they may feel they are floating in space and having weird out-of-body experiences. This may seem intensely spiritual to them, and they may become delirious. Some users report a terrifying feeling of sensory detachment that is likened to a near-death experience. This experience is referred to as the K-hole, a state that has been described as being "pretty much comatose."[10]

Ketamine can cause numbness, nausea, and vomiting. At high doses it can cause delirium, depression, and respiratory depression or even arrest.

GHB—gamma-hydroxybutyrate (G, Grievous Bodily Harm, Easy Lay, Gamma-OH, Liquid X, Liquid Ecstasy, Cherry Meth, Salty Water)

GHB, technically a depressant, is another date-rape drug. While small doses of the drug can produce happy feelings, increased energy, and muscle relaxation, larger doses can cause unconsciousness and other consequences.

Because it is often found in water bottles, GHB can be mistaken for water, but it tastes salty. When slipped into a drink such as soda, the salty taste may be masked. This makes it popular for use in drug rape. The consequences of using GHB can be tragic as this news story shows:

> Date Rape Drug Kills High School Student
>
> Hillory Farias, seventeen, a varsity volleyball player, was found unconscious and not breathing the morning of August 4 after a night out with girlfriends. She died mysteriously by the illegal "date rape drug GHB that was slipped into her drink." She complained of severe headache after coming home from a teenage dance club, where she had two sodas. Authorities suggested that there was nothing to indicate that she willingly took the drug. In addition,

they ruled her death a homicide after finding gamma y-hydroxybutyrate, a "date rape drug" that is known as GHB, Easy Lay, and Liquid X."

—Reported by California State University
at Northridge. Used with permission

Health Effects Although GHB is present in your body naturally in very small amounts, large amounts can produce some really bad effects. Chemically, it is basically floor stripper mixed with drain cleaner.

GHB is often sold in small hotel-size shampoo bottles in concentrated form in which a hit is just a capful. Small doses of the drug can be pleasant, unless there is a bad reaction. Then there can be nausea, vomiting, headache, loss of muscle control, and inability to move. Combining GHB with alcohol or other drugs can cause seizures. Large doses may bring on sleepiness, incoherent and slurred speech, giddiness, unconsciousness, seizures, and death. Passing out while on GHB is sometimes called scooping out, throwing down, or carpeting out. An overdose can mean three or more hours of deep sleep from which a person is not easily awakened, or may never be awakened. There is a long list of deaths from GHB on the Internet.

Ironically, during the 1980s, GHB was sold in health-food stores and by mail order as a nutrient rather than a sedative and was used by body builders to change their ratio of muscle to fat.[11] However, there were so many health problems from it that the Food and Drug Administration (FDA) took it off the market. In 2000, GHB was placed in Schedule I of the Controlled Substance Act along with heroin and the most addictive drugs. Street chemists have taken over the supply and produce it in powder and liquid form. The addictive potential of GHB is not known, but individuals who use it report that they must increase dosage to continue attaining euphoric and relaxing effects.[12]

ROHYPNOL (registered trade name)— flunitrazepam (Roofies, Rophies, Roche, Forget-me Pill)

Although other drugs are used in date rape, Rohypnol is most commonly called the rape drug. Tasteless and odorless, it mixes easily with carbonated drinks and with alcohol. Mixed with alcohol, it has a slightly bitter taste. When slipped into a drink, an unsuspecting girl feels a lot more intoxicated than she would from a single drink and may develop temporary loss of memory. The makers of Rohypnol have reformulated the drug to make it more detectable. When put in a light-colored drink, new Rohypnol turns the liquid blue. In darker-colored drinks, there is a cloudy appearance.

Two common misconceptions about Rohypnol may explain its popularity: First, many young people believe that the drug is unadulterated because it comes in presealed bubble packs; second, many think its use cannot be detected by urinalysis, but this is not the case.[13] Rohypnol is not just a date-rape drug. Young adults have begun using it with alcohol and heroin.[14] This can be a deadly combination.

Health Effects Rohypnol is a depressant that is related to the popular prescription tranquilizer Valium, but it is approximately ten times stronger. Its effects begin within thirty minutes after ingestion and may persist for up to eight hours or more. Like most depressants, Rohypnol can reduce pain and anxiety, relax the muscles, and produce feelings of well-being. However, it causes some users to become excited or aggressive because the nervous system loses natural inhibitions. It can also produce physical and psychological dependence. Once dependence has developed, withdrawal may include symptoms such as muscle pains, seizures, hallucinations, and other unpleasant and dangerous conditions. Withdrawal symptoms can occur a week or more after use has stopped. Treatment for dependence must be gradual, with use tapering off.[15]

METH—methamphetamine (Speed, Crystal, Ice, Shabu, Glass)

Methamphetamine, or meth, is a powerful stimulant with effects similar to cocaine but longer lasting. Meth was a popular street drug in the 1960s and is a popular club drug today where its use has again hit epidemic proportions. Its characteristics were discussed in the previous chapter.

LSD—lysergic acid diethylamide (Acid, Blotter, Dots, Microdots, Sugar Cubes, Trip, Window Glass, Zen)

A sixteen-year-old boy walks along a crowded California beach. He is careful not to touch anyone because he thinks he is an orange that will turn into juice at the slightest touch. He has been using LSD, a drug famous for producing hallucinations. This boy experienced what today is known as a bad trip. The effects of LSD are unpredictable. After his bad experience has worn off, the boy decides never to use LSD again. However, he may have *flashbacks*, recurrences of some of the sensory distortions originally produced by the LSD, that are frightening even though he never uses LSD again.

LSD is a clear, or white, odorless water-soluble substance that is one of the most powerful hallucinogens known. It is another drug that was famous in the sixties and has become popular as a club drug. Today, doses are light compared with those of the sixties, averaging 30 to 50 micrograms rather than 200 or more micrograms used in the past. Lower doses make bad trips less likely.

Some users have a good trip in which sensations may be heightened and common objects or events may become fascinating, appearing as if they had never been seen before. Colors, smells, and sensations may seem highly intensified. They may blend so that the person sees or hears colors and feels sounds. Other users may feel good for part of a trip and bad for another part, and feelings may shift rapidly from euphoria to fear and back to euphoria so fast that the user may seem to experience several emotions at the same time.

The user's personality, mood, expectations, and surroundings appear to play a part in the reaction to LSD. Many users believe that if they feel relaxed, have a friendly guide, and soft lighting, they will have a good trip. This is called setting. However, people who have had so-called perfect conditions have finished their trips in the hospital.

LSD was first synthesized in 1938 in Switzerland where Albert Hofmann, a chemist, was conducting research on possible medical applications of various compounds derived from a fungus that develops on rye grass. Five years after he created LSD, he accidentally ingested a small amount. This is how he describes his experience:

> My surroundings . . . transformed themselves in more terrifying ways. Everything in the room spun around, and the familiar objects and pieces of furniture assumed grotesque, threatening forms. They were in continuous motion, animated, as if driven by an inner restlessness.

Even worse than these demonic transformations of the outer world were the alterations that I perceived in myself, in my inner being. Every exertion of my will, every attempt to put an end to the disintegration of the outer world and the dissolution of my ego, seemed to be wasted effort. A demon had invaded me, had taken possession of my body, mind, and soul.[16]

Health Effects Crystalline LSD is dissolved in alcohol and drops of it are put on sugar cubes or perforated blotter paper, often printed with attractive characters or designs. The drug is usually swallowed, but tiny gelatin capsules are sometimes dropped onto moist body tissue such as in the eye, from which the drug is absorbed. No matter what the dose, LSD is unpredictable.

Trips begin within thirty to ninety minutes of taking LSD and usually last from six to twelve hours. LSD distorts the way the senses work and changes impressions of time and space. LSD users may feel that they have profound insights into their own personalities, their friends, or some aspect of the world. A mathematical engineer believed that he could do problems that normally required three to four hours in fifteen minutes while on a trip. When questioned about his answers later, he said that no one understood him anymore, but that was their problem. Some LSD users experience unpleasant effects that persist long after the trip has ended. Flashbacks may occur after a single experience with the drug. Dramatic mood changes and vivid visual disturbances may last for years and can affect people who have no history of other symptoms of psychological disturbances. Besides affecting the mind, LSD can cause increased body temperature, heart rate, and blood pressure. Some users experience loss of appetite, nausea, sleeplessness, numbness, weakness, and/or tremors.

COCKTAILING

Club drugs are being used by an increasingly broad section of society. Along with an increase in their use, a practice known as cocktailing has become more commonplace. Users combine ecstasy with other drugs such as GHB and ketamine. Or they use alcohol or marijuana to counter the stimulating effects of ecstasy. Some use combinations of Viagra and ecstasy (sextasy). Needless to say, combining drugs increases their risk factors. Death can be the result. Misuse of Viagra is contributing to high-risk sexual behavior.

LSD is not addictive, but tolerance develops rapidly. One of its greatest dangers is loss of judgment and impaired reasoning. People have jumped from great heights thinking they could fly. Others have walked into traffic, believing nothing could hurt them. One girl jumped onto rocks on the beach, believing they had turned into a silky scarf.

Taking LSD has been compared to playing Russian roulette. Some use it with very few unpleasant experiences and seem to delight in the intense colors and hallucinations that occur. Others experience psychotic nightmares that require staying several years in a mental hospital and/or experiencing flashbacks and long-lasting personality changes. People who are prone to mental diseases, such as schizophrenia, can develop the full-blown disease.

CHAPTER 5

PRESCRIPTION DRUGS AND INHALANTS

In the United States up to nine million people may be using prescription drugs, including pain relievers, sedatives, and stimulants, for unapproved nonmedical uses.[1] According to the National Household Survey on Drug Abuse, the most dramatic increases in prescription drug use are among the twelve- to seventeen- and the eighteen- to twenty-five-year-old age groups.[2] Also of concern are the large number of people, especially children, using *inhalants*—compounds that are inhaled to produce a cheap high.

OXYCONTIN (registered trade name)—oxycodone (Oxy, OC)

Ellen is seventeen years old. She lives in a small logging town in rural Maine where she has been an excellent student and a star forward on the varsity basketball team. She lives with her mother. Under normal circumstances, Ellen would be graduating high school next spring. But these are not normal times. Her grades have begun to slip, she has lost weight without dieting, and now she barely speaks to her mother. Last week she was fired from her part-time job as a

A Florida father who is an antidrug activist sits by photographs of his son who died of an OxyContin overdose.

shop clerk because of "financial irregularities." For her failure to appear at team practices, her coach has threatened to drop her from the starting squad. Academically, it is not clear that she will graduate at all. But these many markers of personal decline have not made much of an impression on Ellen. She is one of the many adolescents who abuse prescription drugs to get high.

A minimal user of alcohol and marijuana until three months ago, Ellen would never even have considered trying cocaine or heroin. But when friends suggested she try chewing or snorting a crushed *OxyContin* pill, the idea did not seem so harmful. The rush she felt gave her a sense of power and euphoria like she had never before experienced. Soon Ellen was using stronger doses of OxyContin simply to feel normal. But with no needle marks and no real paraphernalia (except for a small bathroom tile she carries as a pill crusher), Ellen is able to escape detection easily. However, if she misses taking OxyContin for a day or two, she feels awful. So now getting the OxyContin pills, or getting money to buy them, has become a daily obsession.

OxyContin is a prescription drug that has appropriate medical uses when taken under the proper conditions with supervision. OxyContin is an *opioid*, or narcotic, similar to morphine, opium, fentanyl, and heroin. The active chemical in OxyContin is oxycodone, first created in 1916. Oxycodone is an synthetic opioid, meaning it is artificially manufactured rather than naturally grown. The benefits of opioids for pain control have been known since ancient times, but potential for addiction has always been a recognized problem as well. The body contains opioid receptors in the brain, spinal cord, and intestine. When these receptors are occupied by opioids, pain is blocked. There are other pleasurable effects, including euphoria and relief of anxiety.

First approved for sale in the United States in 1995, OxyContin tablets are surrounded by a patented slow-release coating. This innovation allows up to twelve hours of pain relief from a single dose, on a continuous, gradual basis. Because the time of drug activity is so long and the release so gradual, the total oxycodone content of the tablets has to be relatively high. Tablets of 10, 20, 40, 80, and 160 milligrams are made available for use by patients.

That might have been the happy ending of the OxyContin story, except for a simple design flaw, soon discovered by illicit drug users. When OxyContin tablets are crushed, the slow-release mechanism is defeated. The resulting powder produces a swift, intense, and addictive heroin-like pleasure when snorted, swallowed, or mixed with water and injected into a vein.

54

As a drug of abuse, OxyContin is extremely hard to control because it is readily available through domestic manufacture and local pharmacies. There is no need for importation, smuggling, secret farms, or underground chemical factories. OxyContin is produced in the United States legally by Purdue Pharma. Its use is not unlawful, but its misuse, or diversion, is against the law.

Unlike earlier illicit drug epidemics that got started in the inner city or wealthy suburbs, the OxyContin problem began in economically depressed areas such as the Appalachian region and rural New England, far from a metropolis, interstate highway, or the usual international drug-smuggling routes. This is not surprising since these areas have a large elderly population, many of whom are disabled or have sustained injuries with chronic pain from work in mining, farming, or timber industries.[3] Once demand for OxyContin grew among younger users, more and more people got caught up in the illegal trade. Some relatives or economically disadvantaged older patients who had been prescribed the drug by their doctors were willing to sell their pills to dealers at up to ten times the pharmacy cost. Users went to various doctors complaining of pain,[4] so they managed, too, to get multiple prescriptions. Some unscrupulous physicians prescribed OxyContin without performing adequate medical exams or wrote fraudulent prescriptions and split profits with dealers. Blank prescriptions were stolen from medical offices, and in some cases pharmacies were robbed.

With easy availability, the OxyContin epidemic spread like wildfire. It has affected many communities and has now reached the suburbs and cities. Local law enforcement authorities have been swamped with arrests of people who have been found using the drug illegally. By late 2001 forensic medical examiners nationwide agreed that nearly three hundred deaths have been caused by OxyContin over-doses across a two-year period, most often in illicit users who swallowed or chewed the crushed tablets.[5]

Health Effects When used properly, OxyContin has only a few minor side effects such as constipation and dizziness. But an overdose can cause respiratory depression, the most frequent cause of death in cases of opioid overdose.

Many users become physically dependent on the drug and suffer severe withdrawal symptoms if they try to stop, including anxiety, nausea, vomiting, diarrhea, shakiness, muscle pain, cold flashes with goose bumps ("cold turkey"), insomnia, and headache.[6] Some users describe withdrawal as the worst case of the flu you've ever had, multiplied by ten. Many individuals say that they would rather die than endure the three or fours days of symptoms necessary to quit cold turkey, so they go back to drugs to feel better. To help addicted patients get through the difficult withdrawal, some opioid *detoxification* programs place patients under extreme sedation in a hospital.

In 2001 the Food and Drug Administration and the Drug Enforcement Agency took note of the fast-growing problem and issued warnings and advice to physicians aimed at limiting OxyContin use to patients with severe pain. The government also proposed tougher standards for the approval of new drugs in the future, including careful examination for abuse potential. For its part the manufacturer of OxyContin refused to shoulder responsibility for diversion of its drug by criminal elements. The company claimed that its marketing efforts were appropriate and that its drug was safe and effective when used properly. Yet many physicians have stopped prescribing OxyContin under fear of legal oversight, and patient advocates worry about a return to the old days when doctors ignored pain sufferers because they were afraid that patients would become addicted to the drugs they prescribed. Under threat of a $5 billion class action lawsuit by families of OxyContin overdose victims,[7] the manufacturer is proposing a new slow-release formula that cannot be neutralized by crushing. The drugmaker also promises to continue the age-old search for a medicine that will relieve pain without producing the terrible curse of addiction.

RITALIN (registered trade name)— methylphenidate (Chill Pill, Vitamin R, R Ball, Kiddie Cocaine)

Thirty children in a school of five hundred stand in line at the school nurse's office each morning where they will each be given one pill of the prescribed drug *Ritalin* (methylphenidate). They all suffer from attention deficit disorder (ADD) or attention deficit hyperactivity disorder (ADHD), the most commonly diagnosed behavior disorders in children. Children with ADD and ADHD have short attention spans and trouble following instructions, finishing and/or organizing a task, and paying attention to details. Children with ADD daydream excessively. Children with ADHD exhibit many signs of agitation. They fidget and squirm in their seats, act as if they are driven by a motor, and often run about at inappropriate times. Ritalin is the most widely prescribed drug for these children. It increases certain key brain neurotransmitters and helps most of these kids to calm down.

Although numerous studies have been made to discover how Ritalin works and numerous books have been written about ADD and ADHD, much remains to be learned. ADHD is believed to result from the brain's inability to inhibit impulses. Dopamine receptors may fail to register dopamine signals that come in from other neurons. Dopamine transporters, other chemicals in the system that collect dopamine for reuse, may reclaim it before connections are made. The process is far more complicated than this, but medicines like Ritalin are thought to increase the chemicals needed to stimulate the receptors that help people stick to tedious chores and to rein in impulsiveness.

Some doctors think that Ritalin is abused by the medical profession—that many physicians prescribe the drug without carefully examining their young patients. They wonder if the drug isn't prescribed for some children who are just a little immature, spacey, or spirited.

There is another kind of Ritalin abuse, too. Some children grind up Ritalin pills and snort the powder to get high. Where do these children get the Ritalin? Often from children with ADD or ADHD. Take the case of Jacob. His doctor wants him to take Ritalin twice a day, but some of his friends persuade him to sell them his pills so that they can get high. It is possible that many kids like Jacob are not taking all their Ritalin because they can make money selling some of their pills to drug abusers in their classes.

Some children say that Ritalin is as easy to get as candy. But do those who sell Ritalin realize that they run the risk of felony drug charges, the same kind of charges that apply to selling cocaine and methamphetamine? Although Ritalin is a controlled substance that can be legally obtained only by prescription, its abuse through black-market sales is believed to be increasing widely in schools.

For those who abuse Ritalin, the effects are much like meth. Ritalin speeds up the metabolism and can create feelings of exhilaration, energy, and mental alertness. It can also cause psychotic episodes.

Health Effects Ritalin is a stimulant that increases certain key brain neurotransmitters, and this, in turn, increases blood pressure and heart rate, constricts blood vessels, and increases blood glucose.[8] Abuse of Ritalin may cause digestive problems, loss of appetite, weight loss, headaches, strokes, convulsions, and extremely high body temperatures. Since Ritalin contains a chemical that yields dilute hydrochloric acid when it comes in contact with moisture, snorting the drug can damage the delicate tissues that line the nose and can cause open sores in the nose, nosebleeds, and possibly deterioration of the nasal cartilage that separates the nostrils. More than a thousand emergency-room visits have been linked to Ritalin.[9] Abusers seem to become dependent on Ritalin, but it does not appear to be physically addictive.

ANABOLIC STEROIDS ('Roids, Rocket Fuel, Juice, Hype, Pump)

Cheston, a star athlete, was in his senior year in high school when he decided to try anabolic steroids to improve his performance on the football field. Some of his friends were using these drugs to build their muscles and decrease body fat. Cheston bought his supply from a friend, who gave him instructions on how many pills to take. This was many times the dose prescribed for medical conditions, but Cheston was so happy about the improvement in his physical ability that he did not want to hear anything about possible side effects.

Anabolic steroids are man-made prescription drugs that are used to boost muscle tissue and increase body mass. They are used medically to treat conditions such as delayed puberty, and in some cases of impotence, that are caused by abnormally low testosterone production. They are also used to treat body wasting in patients with AIDS and other diseases that result in lean body mass. Anabolic steroids are different from corticosteroids, drugs that reduce inflammation, pain from injury or infection, and are used to treat medical conditions like asthma and arthritis.

Anabolic steroids can be taken orally, injected into muscles, or rubbed into the skin as an ointment. Abusers frequently use two or more kinds of steroids, a practice called *stacking*, in the belief that this will promote larger muscles than larger doses of just one kind would. Another practice used by steroid abusers is *pyramiding*. The person starts with a low dose of the chosen steroid and increases doses for six to twelve weeks. Then the dose is decreased gradually for the next six to twelve weeks until it reaches zero. Sometimes a period in which the person continues to train but takes no drugs follows. Abusers believe pyramiding allows the body to adjust to the high dose, and the following rest cycle gives the body's hormonal system time to recuperate. There is no scientific evidence that shows any benefits of stacking or pyramiding.

Health Effects Long-term use of steroids can cause liver tumors, cancer, fluid retention, high blood pressure, and other problems. In men, it can cause swelling breasts, shrinking testicles, infertility, and increased risk of prostate cancer. In women, long-term use may result in increased facial hair, deepened voice, breast atrophy, and changes or cessation of the menstrual cycle. In adolescents of both sexes, steroid use can cause premature termination of the adolescent growth spurt so that abusers remain shorter than they would have been without the drugs. Acne is often another side effect. The abuse of oral and injectable steroids is also associated with higher risk of heart attack and stroke, and the abuse of most oral steroids is associated with

STRESS AND PRESCRIPTION ABUSE

When people are under stress, they often turn to alcohol and illegal drugs for comfort or relief. Ironically, alcohol and drugs may actually cause more depression and additional health problems.

Even people who have been given prescription drugs by their doctors, such as tranquilizers, sleeping pills, and antidepressants, sometimes abuse drugs. For instance, they might arrange to get prescriptions from a number of different doctors and take them more frequently or in a stronger dose than prescribed.

Tranquilizers and sleeping pills can become addictive, and long-term use can be harmful physically as well as suppress normal feelings. A person who is grieving needs to be able to experience that grief, but pills may suppress normal feelings and extend emotional recovery.

increased risk for liver problems. Steroid abusers who share needles are at risk of contracting HIV/AIDS, hepatitis B and C, and infective endocarditis, a potentially fatal inflammation of the inner lining of the heart.

Steroids can also affect behavior. Abusers may experience a high, increased energy, mood swings, sexual arousal, forgetfulness, and confusion. In addition, steroid use may increase irritability and aggression, although the extent that steroid abuse contributes to violence is not known.

INHALANTS

An inhalant is a chemical that is sniffed for its intoxicating or psychedelic effects. Although sniffing of solvents can happen at any age, this kind of drug abuse is most common among young children. Some start as early as six years old.

The immediate effects of inhaling are similar to the early stages of anesthesia. The user becomes uninhibited and prone to impulsive and risky behavior. The gait is staggered, and speech becomes slurred. The euphoria is frequently accompanied with hallucinations and is followed by drowsiness and sleep.

Children can choose from more than a thousand different inhalants, many of which can be found at home and in school. Solvents are found in such household products as aerosol sprays, cleaning fluids, glue, paint thinner, gasoline, propane, nail polish remover, and correction fluid.

Health Effects No inhalant is safe to inhale at any age, and, in fact, inhalants can and do kill. While drug warnings may seem exaggerated, here are some true cases of *Sudden Sniffing Death Syndrome* (death from sniffing an inhalant):[10] A thirteen-year-old boy was inhaling fumes from cleaning fluid and became ill within minutes. Witnesses alerted his parents, and the victim was rushed to the hospital and placed on life-support systems. Nevertheless, he died twenty-four hours after the incident.

An eleven-year-old boy collapsed in a public bathroom. A butane cigarette lighter fuel container and a plastic bag were found next to him. He also had bottles of correction fluid in his pocket. CPR failed to revive him, and he was pronounced dead.

A fifteen-year-old boy was found unconscious in a backyard. According to his three companions, the group had inhaled gas from a grill propane tank to get high. The victim collapsed shortly after inhaling the gas. He died on the way to the hospital.

While some young users sniff for years, others can die the very first time they try an inhalant. No one knows what will happen. In one study of deaths from inhalant abuse, 22 percent of the abusers who died had no history of previous sniffing.[11] Death can occur in a number of ways. The toxic gases can keep oxygen from getting into the lungs. The users can choke on vomit, or suffocate from lack of oxygen when they use plastic bags over their heads to increase the effect. Or inhalants can cause the heart to overwork, beating rapidly but unevenly until there is a heart attack. Sudden sniffing death can occur during or right after sniffing.

The brain is rich in fatty material, and chronic solvent abuse dissolves brain cells. Sniffing can also severely damage other parts of the body, including liver, heart, and kidneys. When users become dependent on inhalants, they suffer withdrawal when they stop using them.

CHAPTER 6

DRUGS AND THE YOUNG BRAIN

Do you know someone who is pregnant and smokes, drinks, and/or uses other drugs? When a pregnant woman uses drugs, her baby uses them, too. Experts estimate that one half to three quarters of a million babies are born each year after being exposed to one or more illicit drugs. And many more are exposed to nicotine and alcohol.

Although drug-exposed newborns may look like normal babies, they are not. Many are born with physical and psychological problems. Some may suffer behavioral and other effects when they get older. While proper parenting and good health care may help babies overcome the effects of drug exposure, some will suffer the effects of their mother's drug abuse for the rest of their lives.[1]

COCAINE

Elizabeth works in a special nursery for drug-exposed babies where about one quarter of the newborns were exposed to crack cocaine while in their mother's womb. Most of these babies were also exposed to other drugs dur-

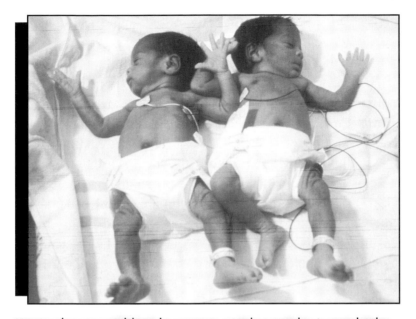

Having become addicted to cocaine in their mother's womb, these babies require hospital care to endure the effects of withdrawal.

ing their mother's pregnancy, including alcohol, marijuana, and nicotine. Many also suffer from malnutrition and other problems, because often pregnant women who abuse drugs don't eat right, don't get proper medical care, and are caught up in a life of violence, degradation, and abuse. Frequently, drug-addicted mothers cannot properly nurture or bond with their infants. All this contributes to the way the baby develops.

Almost all of the babies in the nursery where Elizabeth works are abnormally small, have small heads, and have serious health problems. Many have trouble sucking and are undernourished. Many don't feel well. As a result, some are crying with a high whine while others are trembling and arching their backs. These babies startle easily. Some already exhibit developmental problems. When exposed to the noise of a bell, many fail to follow sound as well as babies who were born without drugs in their systems.

Elizabeth and the other aides who care for the babies try to find time to hold and comfort each one several times a day. For many, that's all the love they get because their mothers are either on the street using drugs or in treatment centers where they are trying to beat their drug habits.

Not all babies whose mothers use cocaine are born with problems, but many suffer behavior problems that may not appear until later in life. Children who are exposed to crack in the womb tend to exhibit behavioral problems that keep them from being successful in the classroom. For instance, they may be unable to block out distractions and to concentrate for long periods of time.[2] Many perform poorly on developmental tests. One study found dramatic effects of prenatal exposure to cocaine in monkeys at a time corresponding to the second trimester in humans. This study showed seemingly permanent reduction in the number of neurons in the cerebral cortex, the area often called the thinking part of the brain.[3] A study conducted by researchers at Case Western Reserve in Cleveland, Ohio, and published in 2002, found that children exposed to cocaine before birth were twice as likely to have significant delays in mental skills when compared with toddlers of similar backgrounds whose mothers had not used cocaine during pregnancy.[4]

Many of these babies are born dead or prematurely. If born too early, many die or have lifelong problems. When babies' brains bleed, there can be permanent paralysis.

Research has dispelled some of the exaggerated fears about infants who were exposed to cocaine before birth.[5] At one time teachers feared that crack kids would be too disruptive to be in traditional classrooms, but much of the disadvantage suffered by the majority of these children is the result of poverty and the use of alcohol and other drugs by their mothers during pregnancy. This does not mean, however, that these babies are as healthy as those who were not exposed to drugs before they were born.

METHAMPHETAMINE

Clinics that treat drug-exposed babies have seen a dramatic increase in the number of babies addicted to methamphetamines beginning in the late 1990s. This alarms health professionals because, while a cocaine high can last for three hours, a meth high can last for twelve hours or more. This longer exposure to drugs may have more damaging effects on unborn babies. While some of their problems may be due to environment, meth babies who were followed for several years continued to have learning disabilities and behavioral problems, such as outbursts of screaming, hitting, and tantrums.[7] Both crack babies and meth babies shake and have tremors. Crack babies begin this at birth, and it is often not resolved until about nine months of age. Meth babies become irritable at about a month after they are born and continue to be irritable for as long as six years.

HEROIN

Babies whose mothers use heroin during pregnancy are often born premature and have low birth weight and smaller than normal head size and length. At birth, the majority also suffer withdrawal as they adjust to living without heroin. Like any heroin addict, they suffer from seizures, tremors, sleep disturbances, and digestive and respiratory troubles. Although these babies appear to have special adjustment and language problems through their first six years of life, lasting differences between these children and children whose mothers did not use drugs have not regularly been found.[8]

OXYCONTIN

With more than five thousand OxyContin emergency-room visits over a period of six months, it is not surprising to find that at least a few of these female patients were pregnant. One mother underwent labor and withdrawal at the same time. Her newborn baby suffered from withdrawal, too, crying hard, shaking, and suffering from fever and convulsions.[9]

During the time that women who are using OxyContin are pregnant, their unborn babies go through cycles of highs and withdrawals along with them. Many of these babies are born early and have low birth weights. With the increase in the illegal use of OxyContin, more "Oxy-addicted" babies are expected, and doctors are studying the babies, watching for developmental problems as they grow.

ECSTASY

On May 1, 2001, researchers from the Children's Hospital Research Foundation in Cincinnati and the University of Cincinnati College of Medicine reported the first evidence that a mother's use of ecstasy during pregnancy may result in specific types of long-term learning and memory impairments in the developing child.[10] Although little is known about its effects on the unborn and experiments have been done only on rats, there is enough evidence to suggest that ecstasy may pose a threat to the unborn, especially if the mother takes it during the early or late third trimester of pregnancy. Since so little is known about the effects of ecstasy on the human fetus, doctors say not using the drug is the only safe way to protect the unborn.

NICOTINE

Exposure to nicotine before birth is far more common than exposure to illicit drugs, and the effects can be serious. Smoking restricts the flow of blood in the arteries and veins, so there is a reduced oxygen supply to the fetus. Smoking increases carbon monoxide in the blood, and this, too, interferes with the blood's ability to distribute oxygen through the body and to the unborn. Studies show that mothers who smoke even a few cigarettes a day give birth to babies who have lower birth weights than those not exposed to cigarette smoke.[11] In addition, there are higher rates of abnormalities in children born to smokers than to nonsmokers.

Pregnant women who smoke put their babies at risk for respiratory difficulties and *Sudden Infant Death Syndrome* (SIDS), the leading cause of death for babies in the first year of life. The U.S. surgeon general has declared smoking the single most important preventable cause of poor pregnancy outcome.[12]

ALCOHOL

Marny, who is three months pregnant, has a few drinks each day. This is much less than her usual amount, and she feels that because she cut down on her drinking, her baby is safe. But each time she drinks a beer, a glass of wine, or a mixed drink, alcohol is quickly absorbed into her bloodstream and continues to circulate until it is completely broken down by her liver. It takes more than an hour for the liver to break down the alcohol in her beer. As it circulates, the alcohol in her bloodstream passes through her placenta to the baby, so each time she has a drink, her unborn baby has a drink, too. Because Marny's unborn baby is much smaller than she is and its systems are still developing, the drinks are more harmful to the baby than to her.

Studies show that alcohol disrupts formation of nerve cells in a baby's brain and that babies born to mothers who drink during pregnancy may be abnormally small, have small heads, and will suffer behavioral and developmental problems as they grow up, such as poor coordination and short attention spans. Yet in spite of efforts to make the public more aware of the risks involved, increasing numbers of women are drinking during pregnancy.[13] The degree to which their babies are affected varies, but at least five thousand infants are born each year in the United States with the disease known as *Fetal Alcohol Syndrome* (FAS).[14] The most severely affected babies suffer many defects, including a characteristic pattern of malformed faces with narrow eyes, low nasal bridges, short upturned noses, and thin upper lips. They may also have heart and joint abnormalities and suffer from various levels of mental retardation.

Doctors do not know how much alcohol is safe for a pregnant woman, so they ask their pregnant patients to avoid it completely. Children do not outgrow FAS, and there is no cure. FAS is the leading preventable cause of mental retardation.

INHALANTS

Sniffing inhalants during pregnancy can cause birth defects similar to ones caused by drinking alcohol, a condition called *Fetal Solvent Syndrome*. There are numerous case reports of mentally retarded children whose mothers sniffed solvent-based paints, glues, thinners, and cements during pregnancy to get high.[15] Brain-damaged babies can suffer from short attention spans, slow growth, damaged nerves and kidneys, facial abnormalities, mental retardation, and other problems. While recreational sniffing is the main cause of Fetal Solvent Syndrome, pregnant women who work in areas where chemical solvents are not properly ventilated may also expose their unborn children to similar risks.

MARIJUANA

Can marijuana use by a pregnant woman endanger her unborn child? Results of experiments with rodents seems to suggest that it can. THC (tetrahydrocannabinol), the principal psychoactive chemical in marijuana, crosses the placenta readily and probably causes low birth weight and premature delivery. Another study indicates that children whose mothers use marijuana during pregnancy suffer developmental problems—they are less able than children of nonusers to focus attention on specific tasks, to plan ahead, and to make thoughtful decisions. But since pot-smoking pregnant women often use other drugs, too, it is difficult to establish the exact effects of marijuana on an unborn child.[16]

THE TEENAGE BRAIN

It has been said that "the young brain is a work in progress," and scientists are now able to demonstrate that this is true. In the year 2000, Dr. Jay Giedd at the National Institute of Mental Health in Bethesda, Maryland, and colleagues at McGill University in Montreal, Canada, reported results of their studies in which they used MRIs (magnetic resonance imaging) to get a close look at the structure of the developing brain. By scanning the brains of children every two years, they tracked the brain's development. Data from MRI brain scans can be used to create three-dimensional time-lapse animations of brains as they mature.[17]

These researchers and others confirmed that different parts of the brain grow at different times. Among the many changes in the teenage brain is a period of structural change, following a gray-matter growth spurt just before puberty. After puberty, a pruning process takes place in the cells of the prefrontal cortex, the part of the brain that controls functions like planning, reasoning, judgment, and impulse control. The prefrontal cortex of the average child matures most between the ages of twelve and twenty, and during this time the brain learns to function more efficiently. Before this maturation process is finished, teens do not have all the brain power they need for making good decisions. This explains why so many teens are prone to making reckless decisions and foolish judgments.

In the adolescent years, teens are establishing their identity as separate from their parents, and peer pressure looms large. Many adults look back at their teen years and remember making bad decisions and being involved in risky behavior that they would not consider as adults.

Teens who constantly rely on drugs to solve their problems miss the chance of learning how to do so without dependence on chemicals. Some young children try marijuana, starting at ten, eleven, and twelve. This often results in the loss of experiences that help children mature. They spend time turning on to drugs that normally would be used learning to cope with problems of growing up and developing social skills. They reach adulthood with the emotional maturity of a preteen.

One man who used drugs through his teen years believes that he missed out on doing a lot of the things he should have been doing when he was young. He feels that his drug use was a colossal waste of time. Now he enjoys natural highs such as finding money in an old coat pocket, watching a favorite team win, walking on the beach at sunrise or sunset, lying in bed listening to the rain, and walking in fresh snow.

CHAPTER 7

DRUG ABUSERS, YOU, AND SOCIETY

Substance abuse causes more deaths, illnesses, and disabilities than any other preventable health condition.[1] It affects people from all walks of life. Even if you never abuse drugs, your life is affected by those who do. The smoke from the next section in the restaurant, the erratic driving of a drunk on the road, and the amount of health care needed for drug abusers are just a few ways that drug abuse affects you. Much heartbreak in families, trouble in the workplace, and problems in the community and in the nation stem from drug abuse. More money is spent on illegal drugs than on art or higher education.[2] When social and health costs are included, drug abuse costs society $110 billion a year.[3] Some estimates are even greater.

VIOLENCE AND CRIME—HERE, THERE, AND EVERYWHERE

From pole to pole and around the globe, people use drugs, and drug use often leads to violence and crime far beyond the users. Alcohol and other drugs, sometimes used separately and sometimes together, are responsible for many

A drug deal goes down.

violent crimes. While many drug users get mellow or slip into sleep after using drugs, others become aggressive both in their drug seeking and in getting along with others. People high on alcohol or other drugs have impaired reasoning and perceptions. This often leads them to do risky things. The person who drives when drunk or high can kill. In addition, drug use leads to other kinds of accidents at home, in the workplace, and at play.

Millions of people lose jobs each year because drugs change their behavior. Substance abuse can create hazards for the employees who use drugs and also for their coworkers. Drug abusers may suffer from accidents, poor work reports, and the problem of absenteeism.

If you live in an area where crack was once common, you may know that crack caused many tragedies and wasted many lives in the past. Crack was one of the drugs responsible for violence by addicts who robbed to get money for their addiction. Crack continues to cause problems, but at a lower rate than in the past.

In the middle of the last decade, approximately half of state prison inmates and 40 percent of federal prisoners who were convicted of violent crimes had been drinking or taking other drugs at the time of their offense.[4] Up to 60 percent of sexual offenders were drinking at the time of the offense. Research shows that people leaving prison after attending drug-abuse treatment programs are less likely to commit crimes than those who do not.

Drugs are expensive. Many abusers of all kinds of drugs eventually run out of money. Often they then resort to stealing to pay for their habit—from parents, from employers, from neighbors, and from friends. Many young girls turn to prostitution to pay for their drugs. Mothers even sell their children for sex to get drug money. Alcohol and all other drugs of abuse have caused financial ruin and other kinds of heartbreak in families through the years—and they still do.

DRUG WARS

Drug trafficking is big business. In some countries, such as Colombia and Mexico, political factions fight over drug cultivation and/or trafficking, causing a great deal of violence. The *War on Drugs*, or "drug war," is called that in part because of the violence that it causes in the countries that supply drugs and those that use them. Fighting over drug profits has led to numerous crimes in the United States as well, including many turf wars where guns are used and people die.

ECONOMIC COST OF DRUG ABUSE

Billions of dollars

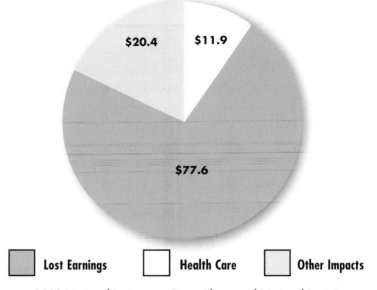

Lost Earnings   Health Care   Other Impacts

Source: 1998 National Institute on Drug Abuse and National Institute on Alcohol Abuse and Alcoholism

Dan was twelve when he began working as a courier for his brother, a drug dealer. Dan delivered small amounts of drugs to buyers. Since he was so young, he was not suspected of drug dealing by the police, but a rival gang found out about a delivery he was making and shot him. He was not killed, but he will never walk again.

Dan knows that some of his cousins work as lookouts and spotters. The lookouts watch while a drug deal is going on and warn about observers. Spotters direct customers to places where they can buy drugs. Both of these jobs are often done by young children, who believe that nothing will happen to them. However, both jobs make kids visible targets for police and for rival gangs, who kill anyone in their way. Young children filling these jobs are often paid partly in cash and partly in drugs. As a result, many become addicted to drugs and need to keep working for dealers to get their supply.

Shotguns and enforcers guard the drug deals and protect the dealer. They collect debts and keep competition away from their territory. If an enforcer shoots a rival gang member who is trying to move in to his territory, he is targeted for a revenge killing. Enforcers usually have short lives. Dealers shoot other dealers in order to control their markets. In some neighborhoods, children are afraid to walk to the store because of drug dealers with guns ready to shoot an enemy. Many drive-by shootings are part of drug violence.

VIOLENCE AND ABUSE AT HOME

Do you know a family who is affected by a member's drug problem? Perhaps you or some of your friends have experienced drug-related violence at home. Elena says her father is wonderful, except when he comes home drunk. Then she hides from him and wishes her mother could do the same because he beats anyone in sight. Her father is always very sorry afterward. Elena's mother has been making excuses for the bruises he made on her face and arms for many years. Until she leaves him or he stops drinking, the violence will continue. Other drugs, such as crack and methamphetamine, also can cause aggressive behavior.

Many incidents of child abuse and neglect are directly related to drug abuse, a problem that is a factor in the placement of more than three quarters of the children entering foster care.[5] Even where children stay in families with a drug abuser, money that should be used for food and education is often spent to support an addiction.

Jack thought he was a good father to his two-year-old daughter, Hannah, even though he was just nineteen years old. He worked hard at his job programming computers and tried to spend extra time with Hannah, especially after her mother left them. But he was under a great deal of pressure at work. He had tried cocaine a few times in high school. Now, he had a chance to get some good stuff that would help him get through the next difficult week. When he got home to Hannah, he could hardly wait to feed her and put her to bed so that he could pour that sparkling white powder on a marble slab, scrape together a few lines of cocaine, and suck it up his nose. What a feeling!

Jack was really high when Hannah called to him from her room for a drink of water, but in his intoxicated state he felt she could wait for the water. After his euphoria wore off, he would take care of her. But Hannah tripped when she got up to get her own water and cut her face. Jack promised himself he would never snort coke at home again. Instead he began snorting at the office and had the baby-sitter put Hannah to bed. His real problems started when his coke habit increased and he started stealing money for the coke and the sitter. Then he lost his job, and little Hannah went into foster care.

The amount of damage caused by drug abuse to individuals, to families, and to society cannot be counted. Children from families where drugs are abused are more likely than other children to exhibit aggressive behavior and bouts of hyperactivity, to perform poorly in school, and to get into trouble. More than 11 million children are adversely affected by parental addiction.[6]

THE TRAGEDY OF JAIL

Many drug users end up going to jail for possession of drugs as well as for selling them to get money to support their habit. In jail, these users suffer their own kind of abuse. Their health and future can be threatened or even destroyed. Two teens who spent time in jail on drug charges described their experiences on a Public Broadcasting System (PBS) special called "In the Mix" as follows:

> Justin: The cells are horrible.
>
> Ashley: The walls are just made up of concrete blocks. And it's real cold in there.
>
> Justin: There are bugs all over the place, the toilets have no seats on them, they're dirty.
>
> Ashley: The beds are so uncomfortable, they're like thin little feather mattresses and feather pillows.
>
> Justin: The showers are cold all the time.
>
> Ashley: I had to sleep with the light on cuz they make fifteen minute checks. . . .[7]

Whole families suffer whenever a father, mother, son, daughter, or sibling spends time in prison. And families of color are more likely than white families to be so impacted. Drug abuse has led to the imprisonment of a disproportionate number of blacks and Hispanics. According to the Federal Household Survey of 1998: "Most current illicit drug users are white. Whites are 72 percent of all users, blacks are 15 percent, and Hispanics 10 percent. And yet blacks constitute 36.8 percent of those arrested for drug violations and Hispanics account for 20.7 percent."[8]

DRUG ABUSE SPREADS DISEASE

Natasha never used drugs, but her husband injected heroin when he was a teen and became infected with HIV/AIDS when he shared a needle with an infected user. Natasha

These two Arizona teens were arrested for trying to smuggle marijuana into the United States from Mexico.

developed the disease after they married, and when their baby was born, she tested positive for it, too.

HIV/AIDS is spreading to more and more women each year, both through heterosexual contact with lovers who inject drugs and through their own intravenous drug use.[9] New drug treatments help to prevent pregnant women from spreading the disease to their babies, but some babies still

HARM REDUCTION

In an attempt at <u>harm reduction</u> (reducing the harm caused by intravenous drug use), needle exchange programs, in which sterile needles are distributed to heroin addicts in exchange for used needles, have been started in some communities. But the practice is controversial. While the U.S. Department of Health and Human Services has endorsed needle exchange programs and there are at least 130 such programs in thirty-one states, they are banned in some communities because many citizens believe that they might increase drug use and crime. In many of these communities harm reduction programs are carried out underground.[10] Gary, whose wife died from AIDS after she was infected by using dirty needles, distributes sterile needles to addicts even though he has been arrested for doing so. He and many others who distribute needles illegally feel strongly that clean-needle programs save people from HIV/AIDS.

Another controversial form of harm reduction is <u>methadone maintenance</u>, a program in which addicts are given methadone in place of a more dangerous drug. Although it is true that this approach substitutes one drug for another, it works well for many former heroin addicts. Brad was a heroin addict for five years and on a waiting list for methadone for two of them. After he was accepted in the program, he did not need to rob stores for money to buy heroin because the methadone he took at the clinic every morning stopped his craving for heroin and prevented withdrawal. With the help of methadone, he is able to hold a full-time job. He looks forward to a productive life in which his heroin addiction is under control.

are born with the infection. Even if these babies escape the virus at birth, many grow up in foster care because their mothers are too sick to care for them.

Intravenous drug users also spread hepatitis C, a serious liver disease that can be silent for many years after the infection takes place. Treatment for hepatitis C is very expensive, and the side effects can be serious.

CHAPTER 8

STARTING AND STOPPING: PREVENTION AND TREATMENT

"We need to prevent drug abuse." Few would disagree with that statement. But finding ways to accomplish this is not so easy and a subject of great controversy. What do you think should be done—educate people about the dangers of drugs, help teens learn to deal with peer pressure, enact tougher drug laws and penalties, establish better treatment programs, reduce the supply of drugs? These are some of the solutions that are part of our nation's drug policy. The effort to reduce the supply of drugs will be discussed in the next chapter.

EDUCATION

Most experts believe that education is vital to fighting the war on drugs. But "Just Say No" programs have not been enough. Nor have some of the scare tactics that have been used. The public service ads showing your brain on drugs as a fried egg did not survive a reality check. The 1947 film *Reefer Madness* didn't do the job either. Produced as an attempt to scare young people away from marijuana, the movie tells the story of how "one puff of pot can lead clean-

Most experts believe that one answer to the nation's drug problem is education. These teen girls are doing their part to educate others about the dangers of using drugs.

cut teen-agers down the road to insanity, criminality, and death." Rather than preventing drug use, the film became a cult comedy for later generations who knew that marijuana was not as wildly dangerous as the film portrayed.

Some new approaches based on science and truth appear to be helping to change teen attitudes about drugs.[1] A widespread program known as DARE (Drug and Alcohol Resistance Education) that was used in most of the nation's public schools is being revised in an attempt to make it more effective. The importance of parents and families in preventing drug abuse is being recognized and encouraged. Experts believe new antidrug campaigns have mixed results. They may deter some teens but encourage others to use drugs. Certainly, some of the new media messages are a far cry from the scare tactics of old. These new radio, TV, and print ads must be honest to be effective.

A newspaper supplement titled "Majority Rules: Most Kids Don't Use Drugs" was distributed through newspapers across the country. Public-service spots aimed at preventing drug abuse were aired on programs showing games of the National Football League and on programs such as Super Bowl and Pro Bowl specials.

Although little sound bites and slogans can help to build awareness and reduce use, drug policy is a complex and multifaceted issue. Most experts believe that it will take more than short messages to convince many young people to avoid drugs. Drug education must be thoughtful, open, and truthful, and it must involve the whole community— parents, schools, police, business—before it will work. Many address the problem of substance abuse by strengthening families and neighborhoods.

Some kids think it is cool to use drugs because they hear songs about them and see them being used on TV and in the movies. They see some of their friends using drugs and assume "everybody's doing it." They assume incorrectly. Many teens who think they must use drugs in their efforts to make friends and fit in do not realize that the percentage of teens who do use drugs is actually quite low. This is especially true if one does not factor in beer and cigarettes. While drug abusers make the news, most young people do not use illegal drugs.

Education about what drugs do and don't do helps people to avoid drug abuse. And the earlier kids learn about drugs, the better. A high proportion of students who experiment with drugs before they graduate from high school continue using them. Among those who have ever tried cigarettes, 85.7 percent are still smoking in twelfth grade. Among those who have ever been drunk, 83.3 percent are still getting drunk in twelfth grade. And for those who have ever tried marijuana, 76.4 percent are still using it in twelfth grade.[2] So it is vital that kids learn the facts about drugs before they begin experimenting with them.

A NEW LOOK AT GATEWAY DRUGS

According to Joseph A. Califano Jr., president of The National Center on Addiction and Substance Abuse (CASA) at Columbia University, there is a statistical relationship between smoking, drinking, and using marijuana and the move to harder drugs. Recently, scientists have found that all illicit drugs, as well as beer and cigarettes that are illegal for children, similarly affect the levels of dopamine in the brain. It is almost impossible to find a teen on marijuana or harder drugs who didn't start with cigarettes and beer.

Dr. Califano believes that reducing the initiation of teens to smoking and drinking would play a major role in reducing the use of other drugs.[3] Teens learn how to inhale tobacco smoke before smoking pot. So nicotine and alcohol are the most common gateway drugs.

Peer Pressure

Many parents think of a pusher as a shadowy dealer lurking outside a school, but most kids start using drugs because their friends or brothers and sisters get them to use them. Handling peer pressure is difficult, especially if one has not planned ways to reject it. But knowing that most kids don't use drugs and learning some ways to reject peer pressure to use drugs can help. Here are some ideas that work:

1. Say no to pushers and show that you mean it.

2. Use one of the following excuses:

    No way. I love my brain cells.

    You're kidding, right? That would be dumb.

    I have to finish a paper.

    No way, man. Taking drugs is not for me.

    I don't want to blow my scholarship.

    Can't do it. Gotta get home.

    I'm grounded.

    I'm not in the mood.

    I don't feel well.

    Marijuana gives me a headache.

    My coach threatened to give me a drug test.

No thanks.

I'm cool the way I am.

3. Choose friends wisely. This is a first step in avoiding pressure to use drugs. Hang out with people who disapprove of drugs.

4. Make your own decisions and follow them. Strong convictions can help you resist peer pressure.

5. Seek strength in numbers. Having just one friend around to back you up can help you refuse drugs, even if everyone else in the group is using them.

6. Don't go places where you think drugs will be used.

7. Don't do anything against your better judgment because you want to fit in. Real friends don't hassle you or ostracize you for your decision not to use drugs.

8. Participating in sports, community, and religion-based activities are good alternatives to drugs.

The great majority of people who experiment with these drugs do not go on to heroin or other hard drugs, but the use of marijuana, alcohol, and nicotine early in life increases the probability that a person will go on to use other drugs.[4] According to CASA, an individual who gets through age twenty-one without smoking, abusing alcohol, or using other illegal drugs is virtually certain never to do so.[5] That makes the need for education all the more important.

DRUG LAWS AND LAW ENFORCEMENT

Although the United States comprises less than 5 percent of the world's population, it is believed to consume nearly half of the world's illegal drugs.[6] One approach to decreasing drug abuse is the threat of jail and/or other penalties.

The challenges facing law enforcement agencies to crack down on drug dealers are daunting. Most states have enacted laws to create drug-free school zones. Stiff penalties are imposed for anyone selling or using drugs within a thousand feet of a school, in a park, or other public area. This helps to give students a place where they can play without being threatened by drug users and dealers. These laws are not always enforced, but cooperation among law enforcement agents, school personnel, parents, students, and local residents helps to keep the school zones drug free.

Equally daunting is the task of prosecuting and incarcerating drug abusers. At present it is against the law for anyone to use a scheduled drug unless the person has a doctor's prescription. Penalties for using drugs vary from fines to jail time. While these laws keep many people from using drugs, many teens use them anyway, most of them figuring they won't get caught. Others have no idea that they are risking prison sentences. Kids who use and sell drugs may find themselves with long prison sentences, depending on which drug is involved. Punishments vary widely according to state laws, amount of the drug involved, whether the offense was using or selling, whether or not it was a first-time offense, and the opinion of the judge who tries the case.

The get-tough approach that produced increasingly harsh penalties for drug abusers still exists in many places. It may have helped to reduce crime, but it has more than doubled the prison population and drained state budgets.[7]

TREATMENT

Drug addiction is typically a chronic disease, and giving up drugs is not easy. Have you ever tried staying on a diet? Dr. Califano suggests that it is a million times harder to give up a drug once the brain has flipped on the addiction switch than to lose weight by dieting.[8] Dr. Califano and many other experts believe that people who abuse drugs require treatment, not jail. And sometimes this means long-term and even repeated treatment to get off drugs. There is no "magic bullet" for treating all forms of drug abuse, or even for treating one form, but despite media reports to the contrary, for many addicts treatment can and does work. Researchers have found that drug treatment programs cut overall drug use in half and cut arrests by two thirds.[9]

Media reports of relapses of famous people who have been in treatment for drug abuse seem to support the false claim that drug abusers cannot be rehabilitated. However, this is not true. In many such cases addicted actors and athletes are urged to return to their work too soon.

Locking up addicts without providing treatment often means that they return to drugs as soon as they are released. Many have no money and no job or home to return to, so they begin using and dealing within a few weeks of their

Drug Schedules

The government groups drugs into five schedules, more or less according to their addiction potential. Schedule I includes those drugs that have a high potential for abuse, while Schedule V includes the least-addictive drugs. These schedules change from time to time. For example, after two girls died from unknowingly ingesting GHB, this drug was moved to Schedule I.

- Schedule I drugs, which include LSD, heroin, marijuana, and GHB, have a high potential for abuse and no currently accepted medical use in treatment in the United States. (The presence of marijuana in Schedule I is the subject of much controversy.) There is a lack of accepted safe use of the drug under medical supervision.

- Schedule II drugs, which include cocaine and methamphetamines, have a high potential for abuse and a currently accepted medical use in treatment in the United States or a currently accepted medical use with severe restrictions. Abuse of the drug may lead to severe *psychological* or *physical dependence*.

- Schedule III drugs have a potential for abuse less than the drugs in Schedules I and II and have a currently accepted medical use in treatment in the United States. Abuse of the drug may lead to moderate or low physical dependence or high psychological dependence.

- Schedule IV drugs, such as Rohypnol, have a low potential for abuse relative to the drugs or other substances in Schedule II and have a currently accepted medical use in treatment in the United States. Abuse of the drug may lead to limited physical dependence or psychological dependence relative to the drugs or other substances in Schedule III. They are legal only if prescribed by a doctor.

- Schedule V drugs have a low potential for abuse relative to the drugs or other substances in Schedule IV and have a currently accepted medical use in treatment in the United States. Abuse of the drug may lead to limited physical dependence or psychological dependence relative to the drugs or other substances in Schedule IV.

The laws for different drugs vary, but those in the first schedules carry the most serious punishment. Although laws vary according to conditions and person, most drugs of abuse, with the exception of alcohol and nicotine, are illegal today. Even alcohol and nicotine are restricted from sale to the young. However, the black market for drugs is a huge supermarket found in schools, on the street, in business offices, and almost anywhere.

release. Recovery is a lifelong challenge, and short treatment programs are often not enough to help an addict stay clean. Halfway houses play a valuable part in helping addicts adjust to living without drugs.

Unfortunately, there are not enough treatment programs for drug abusers in or out of prison. Drug treatment programs are expensive and chronically underfunded. Part of the problem of getting funding for treatment involves the stigma attached to drug abuse. Some communities look at addiction to alcohol and addiction to other drugs very differently. Consider two brothers who are drug abusers and have to appear before a judge. One is an alcoholic and the other uses heroin. The alcoholic is sent to a treatment center, and the heroin user goes to jail, where he gets no treatment. According to some people, the alcoholic suffers from a medical problem, and the other has a criminal problem. According to others, both brothers are suffering from a disease of drug addiction.

When hard-core addicts stay in residential treatment for twelve to eighteen months, there has been great success. When addiction is treated early, it is easier to break. Experts on drug addiction have been arguing for years that long prison terms for nonviolent drug offenders are less effective and more expensive than treatment programs.

In 2001 it was estimated that less than half of the hard-core users of illegal drugs were receiving any treatment.[10] Many people are still being turned away from clinics when they apply for help. Senator Barbara Boxer (D-California) has pointed out that to be turned away when you need help for a serious addiction is very, very deadly. It's deadly to the individual, to his or her family, and to society.[11]

But a number of new programs are under way to improve the situation. A nationwide movement is taking

An important part of drug rehab is counseling. Here a group of teen drug users meets with a counselor.

hold that focuses on treatment for nonviolent drug offenders rather than prison.[12] In June 2000, New York State announced that nearly all drug addicts who are not violent criminals would be offered treatment instead of jail time, with a program to be fully in place by 2003. In November 2000, California began requiring the state to direct most people convicted of nonviolent drug possession into treatment programs rather than prison. However, about 40 percent of those in the program left, and some went back to drug use. Since there was no money for drug testing, addicts could continue to use drugs without detection. And treatment to help them adjust to a new way of life was limited, so there was not much motivation to stop using drugs. The success of these programs and those in other states depends on ways to motivate participants and the amount of funding available.

Nineteen-year-old Dante was a drug addict who was arrested for possession of meth. One night he bought his drugs from an undercover agent who was supposed to be a friend of his supplier, and that was the beginning of a big change in his life. His name was in the paper, he was fingerprinted, and his photo became part of a criminal history record. He could have gone to prison, but he was given three years probation, some community service, a permanent criminal record, and was sent to a treatment program. Rehab could last as long as three years, but if things went well he would be out in one.

At first, Dante hated the rehab center. All the people around him looked wasted, but he had to admit that he didn't look any better. He went through a period of detoxification, then he felt well enough to eat his meals in the dining room. The food was terrible, but he started to make some friends and felt somewhat better. He realized he had a problem, and after a few weeks without drugs and with counseling, he stopped blaming others for his problems. He attended compulsory lectures where he learned about addiction and ways to overcome it. He was assigned to jobs, such as cleaning bathrooms, doing dishes, and working in the laundry. Gradually, some of the other people in the program became his friends. They were very supportive, since each had more or less the same problems. Dante didn't feel alone anymore. He felt accepted. After weeks of counseling, he was beginning to change. He no longer spent time wishing he could manage to get a fix. There was a good chance that Dante would be ready to leave by the end of a year.

A nationwide project called "Demand Treatment!" has been organized by Join Together, The National Institute on Drug Abuse, and other organizations. It aims to increase the number of people who get brief alcohol and other drug counseling and who get quality treatment in communities throughout the United States. This program encourages family members, consumers, and key civic leaders to drive up the demand for treatment through advertising and education in print and electronic media, by large screening programs, by changing public and private policies about drug abuse, and other methods.

Another approach to providing treatment for addicts is the introduction of *drug courts*. These are special courts that handle cases involving drug-addicted offenders through extensive supervision and treatment programs. They use a carrot-and-stick approach, combining treatment with the "stick" of jail. About a thousand drug courts are playing a part in the nation's response to drug-related crime.

Mavis was assigned to a drug court and entered a program immediately after her arrest for using *speedballs*, a combination of heroin and cocaine. She had sessions with counselors several times a week and got support from both her defense and prosecuting attorneys. Each week she appeared before the judge who encouraged her and commended her for her progress. When she slipped into drug use again, she was sent back to jail for a day. Next time she "screwed up," she would go back to jail for a longer period of time. Mavis was sure this would not happen, but it took a number of jail stays before she was able to graduate from the program. In drug court programs, the sanction of jail is used not as a punishment but as a tool to motivate addicts to stay in treatment. Many prosecutors believe that treatment entered under fear of going to prison is more effective than purely voluntary treatment.[13]

Many heroin addicts are in treatment programs that work. People who attend methadone clinics get a daily dose of the drug that allows them to function normally and work

RISKY BEHAVIOR

Addicts engage in risky behavior when they need a drug. A twenty-five year old drives to Harlem from New Jersey. She parks her car illegally on 125th Street in New York City. She is sure it will not be there long, only for the short time it will take her to buy heroin from her regular supplier. But the police spot the illegally parked car, watch her get in the driver's seat, and find the drugs she has just bought. She goes to jail where she suffers nearly unbearable withdrawal pains.

at their jobs. The cost can range from $50 to $150 a week, but it is cheaper than a long stay in the hospital for withdrawal and better than dealing with heroin craving and the need to find supplies illegally. Some heroin addicts stay in methadone maintenance programs for years, where they receive counseling along with the drug. Although it is not a cure, it does enable addicts to live a normal life. Researchers continue to look for effective ways to manage addictions to other drugs.

Addiction stigma keeps some people from seeking treatment even where it is available. Many people suffering from alcohol and/or other drug problems and those in recovery are often ostracized, discriminated against, and deprived of basic human rights.

Bronson was a coke addict who was aware that his habit was ruining his life, so he hid it from his family and friends as long as he could. Bronson wanted to get help, but when he thought about how disappointed his parents would be if they discovered that he was a drug abuser, he decided not to make his problem known to anyone. But when his habit grew severe, he had to go to a rehab center. Early intervention would have helped with his recovery.[14]

Whether treatment is provided under fear of going to prison or is voluntary, it is a very important part of the effort to reduce drug abuse. Some states, such as California, New York, Arizona, and Massachusetts, reported a decrease in the rate in the number of people sent to prison after they began introducing drug-treatment and alternative sentencing programs for nonviolent drug offenders.[15]

Many different kinds of treatment programs help addicts today, but not all of them keep people drug free after the treatment stops. The hunt for new and better addiction treatments is widespread. The National Institute for Drug Abuse is conducting more than sixty clinical testing programs for cocaine and *opiate* abuse alone.[16] Research laboratories in universities and pharmaceutical houses add to the number. Someday there may be vaccines against addiction.

Although the attitude about drug addicts in the United States is moving toward the need for treatment rather than punishment, the bulk of the federal government's drug-fighting budget is still spent on trying to keep drugs from entering the country and on enforcing the laws.

CHAPTER 9

REDUCING THE SUPPLY

The United States is the world's largest consumer of illicit drugs. Americans probably consume more drugs per person than most other countries.[1] While figures vary, an estimated $62.5 billion is spent by Americans each year on illicit drugs.[2] Where do these illicit drugs come from? Some drugs, such as LSD, methamphetamine, and steroids, are produced mainly in the United States, and huge amounts of drugs come into the United States from other parts of the world.

Afghanistan, the Bahamas, Bolivia, Brazil, China, Colombia, Dominican Republic, Ecuador, Guatemala, India, Jamaica, Laos, Mexico, Nigeria, Pakistan, Panama, Paraguay, Peru, Thailand, Venezuela, and Vietnam are deeply involved in drug trafficking and production.[3] Coca production in Colombia has soared in the last decade, and the Colombian *opium* poppy crop has become a source of the heroin seized in the United States.[4] The Golden Triangle (Myanmar [Burma], Laos, and Thailand) and the Golden Crescent (Pakistan, Iran, and Afghanistan) have been profiting from the abuse of heroin in other countries for years.

A DEA agent guards 5,137 pounds (2,330 kilograms) of cocaine confiscated from a Panamanian vessel.

One of the ways the United States fights the nation's drug problem is by trying to reduce the supply. That involves stamping out drug production at its source here and abroad and halting the flow of drugs across the nation's borders. But this is a gigantic task. Drugs are big business. The international illicit drug business generates as much as $400 billion in trade annually. The drug business amounts to 8 percent of all international trade, according to a United Nations study.[5]

The increasing sophistication of drug-trafficking organizations and the ease with which drug traffickers can get automatic weapons make drug law enforcement more difficult and dangerous than ever before. Some undercover officers, Drug Enforcement Administration (DEA) agents, and others in law enforcement risk their lives trying to lower the supply of drugs.

THE INTERNATIONAL DRUG TRADE

The international trade in drugs is complex and involves many people, from the farmers who grow the crops to the dealers who sell the drugs. For example, the farmer who grows coca sells it on the black market to someone who turns it into cocaine. Another buyer smuggles it into the United States, where it goes through a number of hands before it is offered to the users. Each time it exchanges hands, large profits make the price of even a small amount of cocaine many times what it originally cost. Demand for drugs keeps the price high. Law enforcement agencies in the countries where the drugs are grown, where they change hands, and where the users buy them all try to stop the supplies and frequently succeed.

The illegal drug market in the United States is one of the most profitable in the world. It attracts the most ruthless, sophisticated, and aggressive drug traffickers.[6] The most significant drug syndicates operating today are far more powerful and violent than any of the other organized criminal groups in the previous history of American law enforcement.

Today's drug-trafficking organizations have the capacity to overwhelm the defenses of individual nations. Countries can amass billions of dollars in illicit profits from drugs, operating in a number of different countries. For example, drugs from Colombia can be shipped to Mexico and put in a warehouse there for temporary storage. Then they are repackaged and shipped by various methods to the United States. Cocaine may go from Mexico to Europe in exchange for ecstasy that returns to Mexico and is smuggled into the United States.

Drug kingpins in the United States, Mexico, and many countries profit tremendously from America's drug abuse. Smugglers deal with tons of drugs and make profits in billions of dollars. Americans pay large taxes in attempts to stop drug abuse by seizing shipments, smashing Latin American drug factories, and sweeping drug dealers from the streets.

Huge amounts of money from the drug trade are laundered through complicated systems so that the original source is deeply buried and cannot be found. Money launderers in the United States invest huge sums, often under false names, in real estate, local and foreign banks, and other legitimate businesses. Banks that have no physical presence (shell banks), phone card businesses, and traveler's checks in denominations of thousands and even millions are just some of the ways money is laundered. Professional couriers carry a few million dollars, small amounts in the world of drug profits, for deposits in supposedly reputable banks in the United States, the Caribbean, Switzerland, Lichtenstein, and other countries, and they move accounts frequently. The Internet is used by many money launderers to move funds from place to place.

STAMPING OUT
SOURCES ABROAD

Picture coca growers on small farms in Colombia, who sell their crops as merchandise to buy food and supplies for their families. In some areas the economy of a whole community is based on coca. It is the ticket out of poverty for people who live there.

The government of the United States has been sending money to Colombia since the Nixon administration in efforts to eradicate the production of coca and other drug crops at their source. In Plan Colombia, a two-year program that began in the year 2000, the United States increased the amount of money for aerial spraying of chemicals to destroy coca and opium poppy crops and paying farmers to convert to other crops. Unfortunately, farmers grow so much coca that at times this approach seems hopeless. And there are complaints about what such destruction does to the environment. Another element of Plan Colombia is military aid to combat organizations responsible for drug production.

Many of these small coca farmers are willing to substitute crops such as bananas, rubber, and chocolate if they can get enough help from foreign aid.[7] However, the quest for a profitable crop to compete with coca has a long way to go before coca from small farms in South America no longer finds its way to the cities and rural areas of the United States. America's cocaine habit is fueling an estimated $6-billion industry in Colombia where there are long and bloody conflicts.

The United States also works with other countries in the war against drugs. Before 2000, Afghanistan had produced at least half the world's opium supply of 5,000 tons a year. Much of this was smuggled to Europe, and about 10 percent found its way to the United States as heroin. In 2000, when

Faces in the international drug trade—a family of Bolivian peasants with the coca they have grown.

they were faced with international pressure, the ruling Taliban forbade the growing of poppies for opium. When the farmers were told that it was a sin against the teachings of Islam to grow poppies, almost every farmer complied, cutting down the poppies with scythes until fields were empty. No one dared disobey. The poppies disappeared from the fields, but most experts believe that large supplies of opium and heroin had already been stockpiled in Afghanistan. Some of this stash probably slipped across the borders where it was sold for money to defend the forces of the terrorist leader, Osama bin Laden. Afghan terrorists are said to have used drug money to support their training camps and other activities, including the destruction of the World Trade Center and a part of the Pentagon on September 11, 2001.

With the defeat of the Taliban in the winter of 2001–2002, the planting of poppies in Afghanistan soared again. One farmer, who has ten children and twenty-eight people living in his house, explained that raising poppies is the only way to survive. He can make one hundred times more from opium poppies than from fruits and vegetables.[8] There are no factories, no industries, in Afghanistan where people can earn a living. By the spring of 2002, large fields of poppies bloomed again, but a multimillion-dollar campaign, financed mostly by Western governments, promised poppy farmers money to destroy their crops. Many protested it was not enough, and some farmers harvested their poppy buds early for fear that they would be destroyed.

Some countries, such as Iran, are so hostile to the United States that little can be done to obtain their cooperation in suppressing drug production and trafficking. Thailand and Myanmar (Burma) are too weak to suppress opium production. But many countries around the world cooperate with the United Nations (UN) in efforts to reduce the supply of drugs in their own and other countries with varying degrees of success.

Trying to stamp out the supply of drugs by reducing the source has been compared with punching a pillow. What goes down in one place comes up in another. Cocaine is a case in point. Suppressing coca growing by spraying drugs on the crops in Bolivia has moved some of its production to Colombia. Crop dusters continue to spray herbicides over large plantations of coca in Colombia, but some farmers there have created new fields by destroying trees and other plant life in the Amazon jungle and planting coca in what was supposed to have been nature preserves.

STAMPING OUT SOURCES
AT HOME

In addition to the huge undertaking of trying to stamp out sources abroad, there is the job of dismantling hidden laboratories in the United States that produce drugs such as LSD, PCP, and methamphetamine (meth) and of stopping domestic growers who produce marijuana within the nation.

Meth can be made at home, and labs have popped up in many places around the United States in kitchens and bathrooms of houses, motels, and hotels. Producers are highly mobile and sometimes protect their labs with booby traps to ward off potential intruders. Law enforcement agents, who are especially trained to destroy these labs, must wear protective clothing. Meth can be harmful in another way, too. Thousands of meth cooks dump the toxic chemicals that remain after production into the environment, causing damage there. Chemicals in the cooking kitchens are explosive and have started wildfires, injuring and killing people, including children who happened to be nearby. A number of wildfires in California were caused by an explosion in a meth lab. Some states have enacted laws that increase sanctions when children are injured by chemical residues associated with meth production.[9]

Marijuana is often called weed because it grows so easily. Although illegal, marijuana is considered to be a major cash crop in the United States, with large amounts of money changing hands between growers and a series of buyers who handle it before it reaches the users. The Drug Enforcement Administration cooperates with local agencies nationwide, supporting them financially with millions of dollars in the destruction of marijuana fields. Because of the success of eradication programs, many growers now cultivate plants indoors. In one year (1999), about 3.5 billion outdoor plants and several hundred thousand indoor plants were destroyed.

Many indoor growers use sophisticated techniques, such as computerized irrigation. Others use hydroponics, the growing of plants without soil. Indoor cultivation provides a controlled environment conducive to high-potency marijuana that can be grown year-round. Special fertilizers, insecticides, and genetic engineering are used to enhance the supply. All indoor growers must depend on artificial lighting, but this light gives off heat that can be spotted by the DEA and cooperating agencies. The characteristic heat from large-scale artificial lighting can be detected by devices in law enforcement planes as they fly over the greenhouses where large numbers of marijuana plants are being grown. Still, marijuana, grown in the United States and other countries, continues to be available in huge amounts. Marijuana is available throughout the United States—in cities and their suburbs as well as in rural areas. It continues to be the most abused drug in the nation.

SEALING THE BORDERS

Illegal drugs reach the United States in more ways than one can imagine. The drugs that come by air, land, and sea do so in an untold number of ways. For example, huge tractor trailers carry loads of drugs covered by produce, airplanes carry drugs in their tires, fishing vessels hide drugs among the fish, women "rent" babies so they will look innocent of carrying drugs, and people dressed as priests hide them in hollow Bibles. Large numbers of ecstasy pills travel from the Netherlands and Belgium to various parts of the globe by way of world-renowned seaports, extensive railroad systems, inland waterways, local and international airports, and road transportation companies. In many cases express mail

At a border crossing a U.S. Customs officer and his dog check vehicles for drugs.

and cargo services carry the illegal bundles without knowing their contents.

Men and women who are desperate for money become "mules" or "swallowers" and smuggle drugs into the United States at the risk of their lives. Just before they leave for the United States from the drug-producing country, each mule swallows as many as a hundred pelletlike little balloons or a few condoms filled with heroin or cocaine. These men and women travel by plane to the United States, and after they pass customs, they either vomit or excrete the drugs in front of dealers. They are paid as much as ten thousand dollars, but this is a fraction of the street value of the drugs. If a drug-filled elastic pouch bursts in the digestive system during the journey, the mule absorbs the drug and dies from an overdose. Some carriers have turned up dead near airports with their stomachs ripped open by dealers who salvaged the heroin that was swallowed.[10]

Many more individuals, known as "runners," carry drugs across the border from Mexico. Most run across the open spaces at the border, but some go underground. Since 1998 authorities have found six tunnels that were used to smuggle drugs from Mexico to the United States.[11]

Each year, according to the U.S. Customs Service, 60 million people enter the United States on more than 675,000 commercial and private flights. Another 6 million people come by sea and 370 million by land. The vehicles crossing the borders from Canada and Mexico total about 116 million, and more than 90,000 merchant and passenger ships dock at United States ports. This huge number of crossings makes it difficult for drug law enforcement agencies to seal the country's borders.[12]

Some drug traffickers are Americans who travel to other countries to bring drugs home to sell on the street or to dealers who help them arrange their trips. Even teens have been stopped at borders where they thought they could safely bring drugs through customs.

Some drugs that come into the United States are raw materials for laboratories that will turn them into drugs of abuse. A shipment of bubble gum from Canada may hide a load of a drug used to make methamphetamine. In a period of eleven months, between 2001 and 2002, the U.S. Customs Service seized more than 110 million tablets of a decongestant that is used in making meth.[13] The discovery of this flow of drugs from Canada to the United States brought about joint action from the two countries.

Stemming the flow of drugs is mainly the job of the Drug Enforcement Administration, the Federal Bureau of Investigation (FBI), the U.S. Customs Service, and the U.S. Coast Guard. The Bureau of Alcohol, Tobacco and Firearms (BATF), and the Internal Revenue Service (IRS) also help to stem the flow of drugs.

TERRORISM AND THE ILLICIT DRUG TRADE

A drug user in the United States may not intend to support terrorism, but money spent in buying drugs contributes to an international, destructive system that depends on the dollars spent by drug users to survive. As mentioned earlier, those Afghans who grew opium poppies supplied the source of heroin that was sold to support terrorist groups before September 11, 2001. Drug income is the primary source of revenue for many of the more powerful international terrorist groups around the world. Messages from the media continue to remind drug users that their money supports terrorist activities. Individual decisions about using drugs have real world consequences. According to President George W. Bush, "If you quit drugs you join the fight against terror in America."

The Office of Drug Control Policy, which directs the nation's antidrug efforts, reports that spending on federal drug control policies increased to $19.2 billion in the fiscal year 2001. States, counties, and cities spend still more. The total annual cost of the drug war has been estimated at $66 billion.[14] Illegal drugs cost more than $100 billion each year, when loss from productivity is included.[15]

As long as there is a demand, drugs will continue to be produced in the United States and flow into the country from around the world. In spite of tremendous activity to prevent them, huge amounts of illegal drugs still leak

111

through the borders. George F. Will, *Newsweek* writer, says that interdiction sometimes seems like bailing an ocean with a sieve.[16] Immediately after September 11, 2001, numerous guards were stationed on both the Canadian and Mexican borders to keep out terrorists, and this appeared to greatly decrease the amount of smuggling there.[17] However, the traffickers soon became very active, and large amounts of drugs were confiscated at these borders.

Guarding the land, air, and sea continues to be an unbelievably difficult job.

INTERNATIONAL EFFORTS

Law enforcement agencies work together with many nations around the globe in efforts to deter drugs from reaching the streets of the United States. The Drug Enforcement Administration has seventy-eight offices in countries around the world. This agency, in cooperation with those mentioned earlier in this chapter, remains committed to its primary goal of targeting and arresting the most significant drug traffickers in the world today. These agencies work together in attempts to dismantle the world's most sophisticated drug distribution organizations and reduce the supply of drugs.

Most countries that produce large amounts of illicit drugs try to eradicate them, but many of these countries do not have the resources needed to restrict the supply and do away with trafficking. Today some of the major drug-producing countries such as Mexico and Peru receive financial aid from the United States to help them in their war against drug trafficking.

While many people feel it is important to continue to try to decrease the supply of drugs at their source, others believe the money could be better spent on well-planned operations against trafficking gangs and educational campaigns to prevent the demand by drug users.

CHAPTER 10

SHOULD DRUGS BE LEGALIZED?

Since drugs have destroyed so many lives and have taken a tremendous toll on society, some people feel that it is time to explore new solutions to the drug problem. Would legalizing drugs be a solution? Some people think so.

People who want to legalize drugs suggest that handling drugs the way we do alcohol could reduce drug addiction and all the crime involved with drug trafficking and drug abuse. Many of these people say that drugs have always been used and the urge to get high is part of human nature. Trying to keep drugs away from people hasn't worked so far and likely won't work in the future. Many other Americans believe that legalizing drugs would lead to greater problems than exist now. Should people be free to use drugs even if it harms their bodies and they eventually need public medical care?

Those who favor legalization and those who oppose it both agree that drug use can harm developing brains. Not only can drugs seriously damage adolescent brains, their use by teens inhibits social, emotional, and intellectual development at a time when young people are developing social skills and maturing in other ways.

Thousands of people attend a Boston rally calling for
the legalization of marijuana.

Following are some of the main arguments for and against legalization:

Arguments for Legalization Proponents of legalization question the right of the government to outlaw drugs. Does the government have a right to limit what people do to their own bodies? Some advocates of legalization argue that the government is acting like "big brother" by forbidding them to use drugs.

Supporters of the legalization of drugs claim that the prohibition of drugs has its own harmful consequences. They claim the war on drugs causes more damage than the drugs that people use.

Some of these harms include:

- The shooting of innocent bystanders. Illegal drugs are sold to users by gang members who protect their territory with violence. Many people have been killed just because they were in the wrong place when gun battles were fought.

- The expense of the drug war. Trying to curtail the supply of drugs and prosecuting the hundreds of thousands of nonviolent drug users and sellers diverts billions of dollars from the U.S. treasury in efforts to close the borders to drugs and arrest people who sell, buy, and use drugs. After the terrorist attack on September 11, 2001, many people called for using money spent on the drug war on efforts to quell terrorism.

- The profit margin of drug dealing is so great and corruption so extensive that making headway in cutting off the supply is slow and perhaps impossible.

Reducing the supply of drugs from other countries seems hopeless.

- Some drugs are cheaper and more plentiful today in spite of tremendous efforts to stop them from entering the country. If law enforcement worked, it would make drugs scarce and more expensive, but drugs are still plentiful in the United States. The retail price of heroin is three fifths of its price a decade ago, and cocaine costs half of what it did in the 1980s.[1] If drugs were legal, supply and pricing would be under the control of the government.

- Huge profit margins keep the illegal drug industry flourishing. It can afford to lose some of its profits by seizures of large amounts of drugs and it can still make money. Even drug cartels' battles with authorities are financed by profits from their drug sales. So the present way of fighting drug abuse is a losing battle.

- The expensive attempts at controlling the drug supply have sometimes corrupted police and the law enforcement process. According to Mike Gray in Drug Crazy: "Honest cops everywhere are watching in dismay as their departments are sucked under by payoffs at every level."[2] The huge sums of money involved in drug dealing have corrupted many police who feel they are fighting a war they cannot win.

- No matter what is paid for illegal drugs, one can't be sure of their strength or whether or not they are cut with toxic substances. Some illegal drugs are made in underground labs where purity is not a concern. Heroin, ecstasy, and many other drugs are cut with a variety of chemicals to increase their value. Drug users die not only from impurities in drugs but also from variations in their strength that can cause overdoses. Legalization would put drug manufacturing in the hands of reputable companies who would be responsible for warnings and quality control.

- Laws against drugs keep some addicts from treatment. Many are afraid to admit their problems for fear of being stigmatized. In some cases they could be charged as criminals.

- Courts are clogged with drug cases. Legalization would unclog the court system, reduce official corruption, and make homes and streets safer because drug sales would not be in the hands of violent gang members.

Legalization proponents see these possible benefits of legalization:

- If drugs were legalized, the government could control their sale much as it now controls the sale of alcohol. Many advocates for legalization picture a world in which drugs are sold at state-run stores. With legalization, there would be laws against advertising, and drug selling would be under the control of government agencies that would prohibit sales to children and teens. Use would be better controlled.

- Legalizing drugs could bring large amounts of useful tax money, according to supporters of legalization. Federal and state taxes on distilled spirits (such as whiskey, gin, and vodka) count for about 34 percent of the cost. The tax rate on wine and beer is less.

Taxes on drugs would be paid to the government, but the cost would still be less because the many dealers who take their cut from illegal drugs would be eliminated.

- Prohibition now supplies criminals with about $80 to $100 billion a year. Although no one expects taxes on legitimate drugs to bring nearly that much, they would be a source of revenue that could be used toward education and drug-abuse treatment. This might reduce drug abuse the way education about the bad effects of nicotine is helping to reduce the number of smokers.

PROHIBITION

Smuggling was fairly common in the days of Prohibition when alcohol was outlawed in the United States in the years just after World War I. There is some controversy about whether or not Prohibition worked. It did cause serious problems. Bootlegging, the illegal sales of alcoholic beverages, allowed criminal gangs to get a foothold. Many normally law-abiding adults broke the law to get alcohol, and some of them even made gin in their bathtubs. But studies, based on the prevalence of liver disease, show that there was less alcohol use during Prohibition years.[3]

Arguments Against Legalization Those opposed to legalization counter as follows:

- The health risks that drug abusers take affect society in general. It is a function of the government to protect citizens, since adverse consequences affect society. Few argue against society protecting the public from air and water pollution, toxic substances in food, lead in paint, and so on. The use of seat belts and helmets for motorcyclists are the concern of society since the increased dangers of not using them add to the burden of society. Many people who smoke and drink excessively incur huge medical expenses, and some of this is shouldered by taxpayers.

- The idea of selling other drugs in state stores where alcohol is sold does not appeal to those who oppose legalization. They point out the amount of underage drinking. Making other drugs legal would make them seem more acceptable to teens. Even if advertising were suppressed, the fact that marijuana, cocaine, and heroin were sold legitimately would make them appear safer.

- With legalization, there would be laws against advertising, and drug selling would be under the control of government agencies that would prohibit sales to children and teens. But opponents of legalization point out that these laws are not particularly effective with cigarettes and alcohol at the present time. Although states could make efforts to control the purchase of drugs, many children would manage to get drugs. In spite of laws against purchase, 3 million adolescents smoke and 12 million underage

Americans drink.[4] About 87 percent of American high school seniors have tried alcohol, but only 45 percent have tried marijuana.[5] If drugs were legalized for adults, the black market for teens would continue, but it might be much larger than it is today because teens would consider the drugs socially acceptable.

- Availability of drugs is considered one of the most important factors that lead to student substance abuse. Those against legalization believe availability in state stores would increase the number of addicts of all ages. If marijuana were as available and inexpensive as beer, many more young people might try it.

- There are fears that greater availability and legal acceptability of drugs would greatly increase their use. If drugs were less expensive, easier to obtain, and socially acceptable, more people could be tempted to try them. Imagine what would happen if cocaine cost about as much as a cup of tea. Dr. Joseph A. Califano, chairman and president of the Center on Addiction and Substance Abuse at Columbia University, is quoted as saying that the number of illegal drug users would soar like Jack's beanstalk if marijuana, cocaine, and heroin were as available as Budweiser, Marlboros, and Jack Daniels.[6]

- Sue Rusche of National Families in Action says that legalizing drugs would create legal industries that would advertise and use sophisticated marketing techniques to increase consumption. These industries would contribute to political campaigns to block regulation.[7] Some experts believe that if cocaine were made legal, the number of cocaine addicts could jump beyond the number of alcoholics.[8]

- Smuggling drugs to avoid taxes could be rampant. If state laws varied, people would smuggle from states with low taxes to those with high taxes. This is happening now to some degree with cigarettes and alcohol.

- Everyone agrees that efforts to prevent the use of illegal drugs are very expensive, but there is disagreement about whether or not the drug war is a total failure. Certainly it has not stopped drug use, but there has been progress. The amount of drug use has fallen by half in the past twenty years.[9]

- Legalization might actually cost more money than the war against drugs. In addition to the cost of monitoring drug use and the purity of drugs, there would be expenses in licensing growers, dealers, and importers. Schools and police would need to spend money to see that drugs did not fall into the hands of minors. If drugs were easily available, more drug abuse would create more health problems and medical costs would mount.

- Even limited drug legalization would affect social life. For example, the idea of dining in a café where pot smokers are getting high is disgusting to many individuals. The drugs—alcohol, nicotine, and caffeine—that are now legal for adults do not have the degree of intoxication that most illegal drugs have. Large numbers of people drink in restaurants without becoming intoxicated, and drunks are not socially acceptable even in a bar. People who smoke tobacco are being isolated in public places because of the harm from smoke, not because their appearance or intoxicated state is offensive. Would there be sections in restaurants for pot smokers?

WHICH DRUGS?

When people are asked how they feel about the legalization of drugs, they often reply with the question, "Which drugs?" Many oppose legalizing heroin, cocaine, amphetamines, and most other drugs but think that the laws that put marijuana in a class with heroin and cocaine should be changed, since it appears to cause less harm to the human body than other illegal drugs. Supporters of changing marijuana laws claim it has never caused a death from overdose.

Opponents suggest that marijuana does indeed kill. Consider, they say, the deaths from automobile accidents caused by drivers who are stoned on pot and the long-term effects that are similar to, or worse than, those of tobacco smokers. Even short-term effects can cause problems in judgment. Addiction to marijuana happens to about 10 to 14 percent of users.

While many Americans fear that softening the laws on marijuana would increase the number of users, others feel that the laws about possession of a small amount of marijuana seem unrealistic. For years the National Organization for Reform of Marijuana Laws has been trying to change the laws that put marijuana users in jail and give them a record of criminal conviction. Supporters of decriminalization point out that more than 700,000 Americans were arrested for marijuana violations in 2000. About 88 percent of these arrests were for possession only.[10] Many of the arrests for possession were plea bargained. In these cases those arrests for possession received lower penalties than those arrested for growing or selling marijuana.

IN THE NETHERLANDS

The Dutch people are famous for their lax position on marijuana. Sale and possession of marijuana are misdemeanors, punishable by a fine, but this law is usually overlooked. If you are over eighteen in the Netherlands, you might stand next to a policeman while buying marijuana in a coffee shop and not be stopped. The police do not enforce the law, providing the strict laws of the coffee shop are observed. This means selling to no one under age.

In the Netherlands importing, manufacturing, possessing for sale, and selling hard drugs, such as heroin, cocaine, and amphetamines, remain subject to stiff penalties, but possession of small amounts of any of these drugs, although still a felony, is subject to a lighter fine.

While the Netherlands has been accused of being permissive about drugs, the Dutch policy is not meant to encourage drug use, but to separate the *hard drugs* (heroin, cocaine, etc.) from *soft drugs* (marijuana). The government holds the view that drug use is more a matter of public health and social well-being than one for police and the courts.

Whether or not the coffee-shop approach has increased the use of marijuana depends on which reports you read.[11] The Netherlands has been called the drug capital of the world. There are coffee shops with stores nearby that sell drug paraphernalia, and dealers of hard drugs sometimes approach customers as they leave the coffee shops. Opponents of the Dutch policy admit that it has not led to a massive increase in the use of marijuana by young people, but they do question whether or not this apparent social acceptance will lead to an increase in use in the future.[12]

IN OTHER
EUROPEAN COUNTRIES

Marijuana is much more popular than other drugs in European countries, according to a 2001 report by the European Monitoring Center for Drugs and Drug Addiction. Its use has increased in the last decade, but the percentage of European adults who have tried marijuana is much smaller than for American adults. According to the report, European countries with more liberal drug policies in which marijuana is not a serious offense and those with more restrictive policies have similar prevalence rates.[13]

There has been a recent trend toward decriminalization of marijuana in Europe. Belgium, Portugal, Luxembourg, Italy, and Spain have all changed their laws to decriminalize marijuana. In Italy repeat offenders can lose their passports or their drivers' licenses. In Spain users face fines or treatment referrals. England opened its first marijuana coffeehouse on September 15, 2001.

Many experts feel that a policy of discretionary enforcement would not work in the United States, where racism could be responsible for targeting ethnic minorities. According to Dr. Avram Goldstein of Stanford University, inner-city ethnic minorities would surely be targeted unfairly, while drug use by other segments of the population would be tolerated.[14]

Swedish drug policy remains one of zero tolerance with the long-term goal of a drug-free society. Young Swedes are more curious about drugs and less averse to using them than they were a dozen years ago. While the use of Rohypnol and ecstasy has risen, Sweden is not considered a major illicit drug-producing, -trafficking, or -transit country.

MEDICAL MARIJUANA

Marijuana is generally accepted as being valuable in relieving pain and the unpleasant symptoms of diseases such as cancer, multiple sclerosis, AIDS, glaucoma, and epilepsy. Yet in most of the United States the medical use of marijuana is illegal. However, a nationwide survey by the Pew Research Center in March 2001 indicated that 73 percent of those polled favored the use of *medical marijuana.*[15] Many experts feel that voters do not know enough about the subject to make an informed opinion and more research is needed on the safety and effectiveness of marijuana before it should be accepted for medical use. Research has been limited, but on November 28, 2001, the Drug Enforcement Administration granted final approval to a university study of medical marijuana with the hope of introducing some science into this emotionally charged debate.

The controversy about whether or not medical marijuana should be legal is widespread. Voters in Alaska, California, Colorado, Hawaii, Maine, Nevada, Oregon, and Washington have approved its use. Arizona has passed a law that permits a doctor to prescribe any Schedule I drug (including marijuana). But marijuana has not been approved by authorities who claim they know more than the voters, and federal law still makes it illegal. Obtaining marijuana, even in a state that has made it legal, can be complicated.

On May 14, 2001, a decision of the U. S. Supreme Court upheld the challenge by the federal government against six California distributors, known as buyers' clubs. These groups distribute medical marijuana to large numbers of people who have doctors' recommendations. According to the Supreme Court, marijuana remains in Schedule I because it has no currently acceptable medical use and should remain classified with heroin. This was a blow to those who favor its medical use, but many patients continue to obtain medical marijuana by growing their own. Others get it through friends who buy it illegally, or they obtain it from buyers' clubs that are legal by state law but federally illegal.

Campaigns for compassionate use of medical marijuana continue. The National Academy of Sciences Institute of Medicine released the following statement in 1999: "Until a non-smoked, rapid-onset cannabinoid drug delivery system becomes available, we acknowledge that there is no clear alternative for people suffering from chronic conditions that might be relieved by smoking marijuana, such as pain or AIDS wasting."[16] But the American Medical Association remains neutral, saying that more research is needed on the medicinal use of marijuana before doctors feel comfortable recommending it. Some doctors point out that the patient's dose of marijuana cannot be controlled since the content of THC, the chemical that produces the desired effect, varies in different plants and therefore in different cigarettes. Marijuana contains many chemicals, some of which actually cause cancer after long-term use and suppress the immune system. Some say that marijuana is extremely unattractive to most medical patients.[17] Others claim it is very helpful.

A British drug company, GW Pharmaceuticals, is developing a cannabis-based drug that has the pain-relieving benefits without the "unwanted psychoactive side effects." Another drug, Marinol (dronabinol), contains cannabis, but whether or not it offers as much relief as a marijuana cigarette is debatable. Finding a delivery system as good as the lungs is one of the goals of those who deal with the controversy about lifting restrictions on medical marijuana.

THE CONTROVERSY CONTINUES

Both the uses of marijuana for medicine and for recreation are still a subject of controversy and probably will remain so until more research is done on this drug. In the meantime, seizures of drugs at some of the U.S. borders are setting records. The creativity of the drug traffickers is surprising even to the agents who are trying to close the borders to drugs. The citizens of the United States will continue to argue about the best way to keep drugs out of the country, the best way to keep teens off drugs, and what to do to prevent and treat addiction.

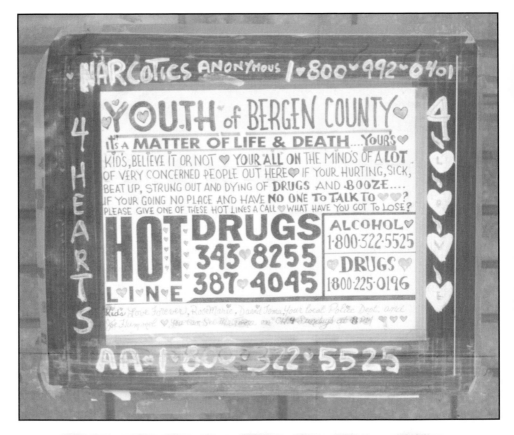

No one needs to face drug addiction alone. Help is available in many places, as this bus stop poster shows.

HELPING A FRIEND WHO ABUSES DRUGS

Maureen and Dantrelle were close friends when they entered high school, but they drifted apart in their junior year. Dantrelle started hanging out with a different group of friends, and smoking marijuana every weekend. After a few months she was smoking daily. She gave up playing soccer and lost interest in her classes. When Maureen found Dantrelle smoking marijuana in the school bathroom before their first class, she decided to try to help her even though she knew that she was not responsible for her friend's problem.

Dantrelle told Maureen that she could stop smoking pot whenever she wanted to, but smoking made her feel better. She said she had planned to stop at the end of last month, but now she has decided to stop at the end of this month. She would not admit that she had a serious drug problem, but denying the problem is typical of drug abusers. They think that addiction cannot happen to them.

Maureen decided to ask her doctor how she could help Dantrelle give up pot. (She could have chosen a counselor, a trusted teacher, or a religious leader for this help.) She kept the name of her friend a secret, even though she knew the doctor would keep their discussion confidential. This is what the doctor told her:

HELPING A FRIEND

Recognizing the problem is a first step. It is difficult for most people to admit that they have a problem, and many will not admit this even to themselves. An addict who is using drugs may not be rational except to rationalize his or her behavior.

Talk to your friend when he or she is not high. Plan ahead what you want to say and how to say it. Choose a quiet and private time to talk. Use a calm voice and don't get into an argument.

Let your friend know that you care. Suggest a local hot line or counseling and offer to go along to a counselor with her. If other friends know that the person has a problem, ask them to speak to him or her, too. **It is not your problem to get your friend to stop using drugs, but the more people who express concern, the better the chances are of your friend getting help.**

Suggest drug-free activities such as sports and other after-school activities. Check your local library and recreation center for more activities and go with your friend. Exercise is a major element in detox programs. It improves physical condition, helps to get rid of nervous energy, and enhances mood. Don't go to raves where drugs are common.

It might be that the best thing you can do is set an example, showing that life can be great without drugs.

If you need help in finding a treatment center, you can find the nearest by searching the Substance Abuse Treatment Facility Locator online at findtreament.samsha.gov/. Or call a hot line listed under For More Information in this book.

Drug Profiles

Source: NCADI 2002 Drugs of Abuse

CANNABIS

DRUG	DEPENDENCE Physical/Psychological	HOW USED	DURATION (hours)
Marijuana	Unknown/Moderate	Smoked, oral	2–4
Tetrahydrocannabinol	Unknown/Moderate	Smoked, oral	2–4
Hashish	Unknown/Moderate	Smoked, oral	2–4
Hashish Oil	Unknown/Moderate	Smoked, oral	2–4

WHAT IS CANNABIS?
Hemp plant from which marijuana and hashish are produced
Hashish consists of resinous secretions of the cannabis plant; marijuana is a tobacco-like substance.

POSSIBLE EFFECTS
Euphoria followed by relaxation
Change in appetite
Impaired memory, concentration, knowledge retention; loss of coordination
More vivid sense of taste, sight, smell, hearing
Stronger doses cause fluctuating emotions, fragmentary thoughts, disoriented behavior, psychosis.
May cause irritation to lungs, respiratory system; may cause cancer

SYMPTOMS OF OVERDOSE
Fatigue, lack of coordination, paranoia, psychosis

WITHDRAWAL SYNDROME
Insomnia, hyperactivity, sometimes change in appetite

INDICATIONS OF POSSIBLE MISUSE
Animated behavior, loud talking, followed by sleepiness
Dilated pupils, bloodshot eyes
Distortions in perception; hallucinations
Distortions in depth and time perception; loss of coordination

DEPRESSANTS

DRUG	DEPENDENCE Physical/Psychological	HOW USED	DURATION (hours)
Barbiturates	High/Moderate	Oral	1–16
Methaqualone	High/High	Oral	4–8
Tranquilizers	High/High	Oral	4–8
Chloral Hydrate	Moderate/Moderate	Oral	5–8
Glutethimide	High/Moderate	Oral	4–8

WHAT ARE DEPRESSANTS?
Drugs used medicinally to relieve anxiety, irritability, tension
High potential for abuse, development of tolerance
Produce state of intoxication similar to that of alcohol
Combined with alcohol, increase effects, multiply risks

POSSIBLE EFFECTS
Sensory alteration, anxiety reduction, intoxication
Small amounts cause calmness, relaxed muscles.
Larger amounts cause slurred speech, impaired judgment, loss of motor coordination.
Very large doses may cause respiratory depression, coma, death.
Newborn babies of abusers may show dependence, withdrawal symptoms, behavioral problems, birth defects.

SYMPTOMS OF OVERDOSE
Shallow respiration, clammy skin, dilated pupils
Weak and rapid pulse, coma, death

WITHDRAWAL SYNDROME
Anxiety, insomnia, muscle tremors, loss of appetite
Abrupt cessation or reduced high dose may cause convulsions, delirium, death.

INDICATIONS OF POSSIBLE MISUSE
Behavior similar to alcohol intoxication (without odor of alcohol on breath)
Staggering, stumbling, lack of coordination, slurred speech
Falling asleep while at work, difficulty concentrating
Dilated pupils

HALLUCINOGENS

DRUG	DEPENDENCE Physical/Psychological	HOW USED	DURATION (hours)
PCP	Unknown/High	Smoked, oral, injected	Up to days
LSD	None/Unknown	Oral	8–12
Mescaline, Peyote	None/Unknown	Oral, injected	8–12
Psilocybin	None/Unknown	Oral, injected, smoked, sniffed	Variable
Designer Drugs*	Unknown/Unknown	Oral, injected, smoked	Variable

*Phencyclidine analogs, amphetamine variants

WHAT ARE HALLUCINOGENS?
Drugs that produce behavioral changes that are often multiple and dramatic
No known medical use, but some block sensation to pain and use may result in self-inflicted injuries
Designer drugs, such as Ecstacy, made specifically in underground laboratories to imitate certain controlled substances and circumvent the scheduling law; are often many times stronger than drugs they imitate

POSSIBLE EFFECTS
Rapidly changing feelings, immediately and long after use
Chronic use may cause persistent problems, depression, violent behavior, anxiety, distorted perception of time.
Large doses may cause convulsions, coma, heart/lung failure, ruptured blood vessels in the brain.
May cause hallucinations, illusions, dizziness, confusion, suspicion, anxiety, loss of control
Delayed effects—"flashbacks" may occur long after use
Designer drugs—one use may cause irreversible brain damage

SYMPTOMS OF OVERDOSE
Longer, more intense "trip" episodes, psychosis, coma, death

WITHDRAWAL SYNDROME
No known withdrawal syndrome

INDICATIONS OF POSSIBLE MISUSE
Extreme changes in behavior and mood; person may sit or recline in a trancelike state; person may appear fearful
Chills, irregular breathing, sweating, trembling hands
Changes in sense of light, hearing, touch, smell, and time
Increase in blood pressure, heart rate and blood sugar

134

NARCOTICS

DRUG	DEPENDENCE Physical/Psychological	HOW USED	DURATION (hours)
Opium	High/High	Oral, smoked	3–6
Morphine	High/High	Oral, smoked, injected	3–6
Codeine	Moderate/Moderate	Oral, injected	3–6
Heroin	High/High	Smoked, injected, sniffed	3–6
Methadone	High/High	Oral, injected	12–24

WHAT ARE NARCOTICS?
Drugs used medicinally to relieve pain
High potential for abuse
Cause relaxation with an immediate "rush"
Initial unpleasant effects—restlessness, nausea

POSSIBLE EFFECTS
Euphoria
Drowsiness, respiratory depression
Constricted (pinpoint) pupils

SYMPTOMS OF OVERDOSE
Slow, shallow breathing, clammy skin
Convulsions, coma, possible death

WITHDRAWAL SYNDROME
Watery eyes, runny nose, yawning, cramps
Loss of appetite, irritability, nausea
Tremors, panic, chills, sweating

INDICATIONS OF POSSIBLE MISUSE
Scars (tracks) caused by injections
Constricted (pinpoint) pupils
Loss of appetite
Sniffles, watery eyes, cough, nausea
Lethargy, drowsiness, nodding
Syringes, bent spoons, needles, etc.

STEROIDS

DRUG	DEPENDENCE Physical/Psychological	HOW USED	DURATION (hours)
Dianabol	Possible/Possible	Oral	Days–Weeks
Nandrolone	Possible/Possible	Oral	Days–Weeks

WHAT ARE STEROIDS?
Synthetic compounds available legally and illegally
Drugs that are closely related to the male sex hormone, testosterone
Moderate potential for abuse, particularly among young males

POSSIBLE EFFECTS
Increase in body weight
Increase in muscle strength
Enhance athletic performance
Increase in physical endurance

SYMPTOMS OF OVERDOSE
Quick weight and muscle gains
Extremely aggressive behavior or "Roid rage"
Severe skin rashes
Impotence, withered testicles
In females, development of irreversible masculine traits

WITHDRAWAL SYNDROME
Significant weight loss
Depression
Behavioral changes
Trembling

INDICATIONS OF POSSIBLE MISUSE
Increased combativeness and aggressiveness
Jaundice
Purple or red spots on body; unexplained darkness of skin
Persistent unpleasant breath odor
Swelling of feet or lower legs

STIMULANTS

DRUG	DEPENDENCE Physical/Psychological	HOW USED	DURATION (hours)
Cocaine*	Possible/High	Sniffed, smoked, injected	1–2
Amphetamines	Possible/High	Oral, injected	2–4
Methamphetamine	Possible/High	Oral, injected; smoked, inhaled (ice)	2–4 4–14
Phenmetrazine	Possible/High	Oral, injected	2–4
Methylphenidate	Possible/Moderate	Oral, injected	2–4
Other Stimulants	Possible/High	Oral, injected	2–4

*Cocaine, while classified under the Controlled Substances Act (CSA) as a narcotic, is also discussed as a stimulant.

WHAT ARE STIMULANTS?
Drugs used to increase alertness, relieve fatigue, feel stronger and more decisive; used for euphoric effects or to counteract the "down" feeling of tranquilizers or alcohol

POSSIBLE EFFECTS
Increased heart and respiratory rates
Elevated blood pressure, dilated pupils, and decreased appetite
High doses may cause rapid or irregular heartbeat, loss of coordination, collapse.
May cause perspiration, blurred vision, dizziness, a feeling of restlessness, anxiety, delusions

SYMPTOMS OF OVERDOSE
Agitation, increase in body temperature, hallucinations, convulsions, possible death

WITHDRAWAL SYNDROME
Apathy, long periods of sleep, irritability, depression, disorientation

INDICATIONS OF POSSIBLE MISUSE
Excessive activity, talkativeness, irritability, argumentativeness or nervousness Increased blood pressure or pulse rate, dilated pupils
Long periods without sleeping or eating
Euphoria

INHALANTS

INCLUDE:

Butyl nitrite

Amyl nitrite (Gas in aerosol cans)

Gasoline and Toluene vapors (Correction fluid, glue, marking pens)

YOU PROBABLY KNOW WHY INHALANTS ARE ABUSED —

Cheap High

Quick buzz

Fun

BUT DID YOU KNOW THAT INHALANTS MAY CAUSE —

Loss of muscle control

Slurred speech

Drowsiness or loss of consciousness

Excessive secretions from the nose and watery eyes

Brain damage and damage to lung cells

GLOSSARY

addiction: a condition in which a user continues to use a drug in spite of harm to self and others, spends excessive time in obtaining the drug, and suffers from increased tolerance to the drug. In some definitions, there is withdrawal when drug use stops.

alcoholic: a person addicted to alcohol.

amphetamines: drugs that stimulate.

anabolic steroids: man-made prescription drugs that are used to boost muscle tissue and increase body mass; can induce growth or thickening of the body's nonreproductive tract tissues (including skeletal muscle, bones, the larynx, and vocal cords) and decrease body fat.

cannabinoids: narcotics produced from the *Cannabis sativa*, hemp plant (marijuana, hashish).

club drug: a hallucinogen or dissociative drug often used at parties.

cocaine: a powerful stimulant found in coca leaves that produces an intense, short-lived high and is very addictive.

cocktailing: using combinations of drugs.

crack: a very potent and highly addictive form of cocaine.

date-rape drug: one of several generally odorless and colorless drugs that predatory males slip into the drinks of females so they can render them unconscious and rape them.

decriminalization: the removal of penalties for possession of drugs for personal use. Small fines may be issued, but there is no arrest, incarceration, or criminal record.

depressants: drugs used medicinally to relieve anxiety, irritability, and tension; produce a state of intoxication similar to that of alcohol and have a high potential for abuse.

designer drug: a drug made in an illicit laboratory to imitate certain controlled substances and circumvent the drug-scheduling law.

detoxification: getting off drugs; breaking a substance down to remove its toxic quality, generally by the liver.

dissociative drugs: drugs that distort perceptions of reality.

dopamine: a neurotransmitter that has many functions. It is thought to regulate emotional response and play a role in the abuse of many kinds of drugs.

drug: any chemical agent that affects biological function.

drug courts: special courts that handle cases involving drug addicts through extensive supervision and treatment programs.

ecstasy: a popular but dangerous club drug that produces feelings of peacefulness and exhilaration; classified as a chemically modified amphetamine that has psychedelic as well as simulative properties.

fetal alcohol syndrome (FAS): a group of symptoms resulting from pregnant women's use of alcohol.

fetal solvent syndrome (FAS): a group of symptoms resulting from pregnant women's use of inhalants.

flashback: a recurrence of sensory distortions originally produced by a drug.

gateway drugs: drugs that lead to the use of other drugs.

GHB (gamma hydroxybutyrate): originally available in health-food stores for body builders, GHB and other synthetic steroids are also used for their euphoric effect. Sometimes used as a date-rape drug.

hallucination: a distorted perception, spaciness, seeing things that are not real.

hallucinogens: drugs that alter perceptions and feelings; some block sensation to pain.

hard drug: term used by some to refer to the most dangerous drugs (heroin, cocaine, etc.)

harm reduction: a way of reducing the harm caused by those people who cannot or will not stop using drugs. It identifies practices and beliefs that endanger individuals and communities and attempts to engage nonjudgmentally with people and to face the harm done to and by them.

hashish: a cannabinoid made from the leaves and stalks of the hemp plant.

heroin: a highly addictive opiate that is made from morphine; produces an intense high followed by sleepiness.

inhalant: any chemical used to produce a high when inhaled. Many are found in common household products, such as paint thinners.

ketamine: a rapid-acting general anesthetic. Produces a wide range of feelings, from weightlessness to out-of-body or near-death experiences.

legalization: repealing drug laws.

LSD (lysergic acid diethylamide): a hallucinogen that produces unpredictable effects depending on the amount taken, the surroundings in which the drug is used, and the user's personality, mood, and expectations.

marijuana: a cannabinoid which is produced from the dried leaves, stems, and flowering tops of the hemp plant.

MDMA (methylenedioxymethamphetamine): commonly known as ecstasy, a drug of choice at raves and parties where young people gather.

medical marijuana: marijuana that is used to reduce pain and increase appetite in patients with cancer, multiple sclerosis, AIDS, and other diseases. Although some states have passed laws approving use, the federal government forbids it.

methadone: a long-acting synthetic medication that is effective in treating addiction to opiates.

methadone maintenance: a form of harm reduction in which addicts are given methadone to wean them off a more dangerous drug.

methamphetamines: powerful stimulants that cause excitation and an extraordinary compulsion to go on using.

narcotics: drugs used medicinally to relieve pain; produce euphoria and thus have a high potential for abuse.

neurotransmitter: a chemical released by neurons at a synapse for the purpose of relaying information by way of receptors.

opiates: narcotics derived from opium, such as morphine and heroin.

opioids: similar to opiate narcotics but not derived from opium.

opium: a narcotic produced from the opium poppy.

OxyContin: an opioid prescribed as a painkiller and abused to provide a heroin-like high.

physical dependence: the body's continuing need for a drug with withdrawal symptoms when the drug is no longer administered.

psychological dependence: an emotional or mental need for a drug.

pyramiding: gradually increasing and then decreasing doses of bodybuilding steroids.

Ritalin: a stimulant used to control attention deficit disorder but abused when taken without a prescription.

Rohypnol: a depressant of the central nervous system that produces muscle relaxation and amnesia. Known as a date-rape drug.

serotonin: a neurotransmitter that plays a role in sensory perception, temperature regulation, onset of sleep, and more.

soft drugs: term used by some to refer to the less addictive drugs such as marijuana.

speedball: a combination of heroin and cocaine.

stacking: using two or more kinds of steroids to create larger muscles.

steroids: prescription drugs abused by bodybuilders.

stimulants: drugs that enhance the activity of the brain and lead to increased heart rate, blood pressure, and respiration.

sudden infant death syndrome (SIDS): also known as crib death. Sudden death of a sleeping baby for which cause is uncertain.

sudden sniffing death syndrome: death from sniffing an inhalant.

tolerance: a condition in which higher doses of a drug are required to produce the same effect as experienced initially.

War on Drugs: campaign to "fight the plague of drugs" launched by President Nixon in 1968 and still official U.S. policy.

withdrawal: a variety of unpleasant and sometimes painful symptoms that occur after the chronic use of some drugs is reduced or stopped.

NOTES

TO OUR READERS: All the Internet addresses in this book were active and correct when the book went to press.

CHAPTER 1

1. CASA National Survey of American Attitudes on Substance Abuse (New York: Columbia University, 2001).
2. Evelyn Nieves, "Heroin, an Old Nemesis, Makes an Encore." *The New York Times*, January 9, 2001.
3. Kris Axtman, "Dangerous Drug Trend: Mixing Substances." *Christian Science Monitor*, August 17, 2001.
4. www.drugabuse.gov/MedAdv/01/NR12-19.html
5. www.health.org/multimedia/webcasts/pdfaecstasy/
6. Constance Horgan, *Substance Abuse: The Nation's Number One Health Problem* (Princeton, NJ: The Robert Wood Johnson Foundation, 2001), p. 8.
7. Horgan, *Substance Abuse*, p. 8.
8. Partnership for a Drug-Free America, "2000 Partnership Attitude Tracking Study (PATS)," November 27, 2001.
9. www.drugfreeamerica.org, and www.smhsa.org
10. National Drug Control Strategy: 2001 Annual Report (Washington, DC: Superintendent of Documents, 2001), p. 56.

CHAPTER 2

1. David Friedman and Sue Rusche, *False Messengers: How Addictive Drugs Change the Brain*. (The Netherlands: Harwood Academic Publishers, 1999), p. 134.
2. Friedman, *False Messengers,* p. 148.
3. Friedman, *False Messengers,* pp. 31–32.
4. www.nida.nih.gov/Testimony/3-19-98Testimony.html
5. Jennifer Hurley, editor, *Addiction: Opposing Viewpoints* (San Diego, CA: Greenhaven Press, 2000), p. 26.
6. www.health.org/govpubs/phd861/index.htm
7. "Discover Dialogue with Molecular Physicist Eric Nestler," *Discover*, October 2001, p. 23.
8. "A Survey of Illegal Drugs," *The Economist*, July 26, 2001, p. 9.
9. Friedman, *False Messengers*, Foreword

CHAPTER 3

1. Sarah Richardson, *Discover*, January 1998, p. 67.
2. Avram Goldstein, *Addiction: From Biology to Drug Policy* (New York: Oxford University Press, 2001), p. 198.
3. David Friedman and Sue Rusche, *False Messengers: How Addictive Drugs Change the Brain*. (The Netherlands: Harwood Academic Publishers, 1999), p. 57.
4. Erica Goode, "For Users of Heroin, Decades of Despair," *The New York Times*, May 22, 2001.
5. www.acde.org/common/Cocaine.htm
6. www.gov/news/pr/may2001/nida-30.htm
7. Daryl Inaba, William E. Cohen, and Michael Holstein, *Uppers, Downers, and All Arounders* (Ashland, OR: CNS Publications, Inc., 1993), p. 107.
8. www.nida.nih.gov/ResearchReports/Methamph/methamph3.html

CHAPTER 4

1. "Violence Rises as Club Drugs Spread Out Into the Streets," *The New York Times*, June 24, 2001.
2. www.clubdrugs.org
3. www.emory.edu/NFIA/about/students/sia6.html
4. www.drugabuse.govNIDA_Notes/NNVol11N5/Ecstasy.html
5. David P. Friedman and Sue Rusche, *False Messengers: How Addictive Drugs Change the Brain* (The Netherlands: Harwood Academic Publishers, 1999), p. 73.

6. www.ncjrs.org/club_drugs/club_drugs.html
7. "Ecstasy Use Rises: What More Needs to Be Done by the Government to Combat This Problem," Hearing Before the Senate Government Affairs Committee, July 30, 2001.
8. From the video *Ecstasy*, produced by "In the Mix," the PBS weekly series for teens. Quoted with permission.
9. *Hallucinogens and Dissociative Drugs*, Research Report, National Institute of Health Publication Number 01-4209, p. 2.
10. www.pbs.org/inthemix/shows/jim/html
11. Daryl Inaba, William Cohen, and Michael Holstein, *Uppers, Downers, and All Arounders* (Ashland, OR: CNS Publications, Inc., 1993), p. 168.
12. Lori Whitten, "Conference Highlights Increasing GHB Abuse" (Bethesda, MD: NIDA Notes, Volume 16, Number 2, May 2001), p. 11.
13. Whitten, "Conference Highlights," p. 11.
14. www.health.org/newsroom/rep/184.htm
15. www.usdoj.gov/dea/concern/rohypnol.htm
16. www.usdoj.gov/dea/concern/rohypnol.htm
17. National Institute of Drug Abuse, Research Report, "Hallucinogens and Dissociate Drugs" (Bethesda, MD: National Institutes of Health, 2001), p. 3.

CHAPTER 5

1. National Institute on Drug Abuse Research Report Series: Prescription Drugs. Research Report, Publication Number 01-4481, 2001, p. 1.
2. A. Spake, "'Not An Appropriate Use,' Did the Makers of OxyContin Push Too Hard?" *US News & World Report*, July 2, 2001, p. 26.
3. M. Sappenfield, "Rise of 'Hillbilly Heroin' Creates Alarm in East," *Christian Science Monitor*, July 12, 2001, p.1.
4. B. Meier, "Overdoses of Painkiller Are Linked to 282 Deaths," *The New York Times*, October 28, 2001.
5. Meier, "Overdoses of Painkiller."
6. D. Rosenberg, "Profits vs. Pain Relief," *Newsweek*, July 2, 2001, p. 49.
7. Research Report Series, "Prescription Drugs: Abuse and Addiction" (Washington, DC: National Institute on Drug Abuse, 2001), p. 4.
8. Eileen Beal, *Ritalin: Its Use and Abuse* (New York: The Rosen Publishing Group, 1999), p. 37.

9. www.ahealth.com/Consumer/disorders/InhalantAb.html
10. www.aap.org/policy/re9609.html

CHAPTER 6
1. www.brown.edu/Administration/George_Street_Journal/new-borns.html
2. www.nida.gov/researchreports/cocaine/cocaine4.html
3. "No Time for Complacency: The Fetal Brain on Drugs," *Journal of Comparative Neurology*, August 2001, pp. 256–269.
4. 165.112.78.61/MedAdv/02/NR4-19.htm
5. "Study Finds Tales of 'Crack Babies' Exaggerated," *Journal of the America Medical Association*, March 27, 2001, p. 1613.
6. "Study Finds," p. 1613.
7. www.odyssey.on.ca/~balancebeam/Health/meth.htm
8. babyparenting.about.com/library/blDBheroin.htm
9. Debra Rosenberg, "Oxy's Offspring," *Newsweek*, April 22, 2002, p. 37.
10. Harry Broening and others, "Ecstasy-induced Learning and Memory Impairment Depend on the Age of Exposure During Early Development," *The Journal of Neuroscience*, May 1, 2001, vol. 21(9), pp. 3228–3235.
11. "Cut It Out," *New Scientist*, October 20, 2001, p. 29.
12. Constance Horgan, *Substance Abuse: The Nation's Number One Health Problem* (Princeton, NJ: Robert Wood Johnson Foundation, 2001), p. 48.
13. babyparenting.about.com/library/weekly/aa010199.htm
14. Nels Erison, "Substance Abuse: The Nation's Number One Health Problem" (Washington, DC: Office of Justice Programs Fact Sheet Number FS-2000117, May 2001), unpaged.
15. Avram Goldstein, *Addiction* (New York: Oxford University Press, 2001), p. 203.
16. aging.healthlink.mcw.edu/article/982087834.html
17. Horgan, *Substance Abuse*, p. 4
18. Office of National Drug Control Policy, National Drug Control Strategy, Annual Report 2001 (Washington, DC: U.S. Government Printing Office, 2001), p. 56.

CHAPTER 7
1. Office of National Drug Control Policy, National Drug Control Strategy, Annual Report 2001 (Washington, DC: U.S. Government Printing Office, 2001), p. 56.
2. Constance Horgan, *Substance Abuse: The Nation's Number*

One Health Problem (Princeton, NJ: Robert Wood Johnson Foundation, 2001), p. 66.

3. Horgan, *Substance Abuse,* p. 64.
4. *Help For Kids Whose Parents Use Drugs*, Update, National Youth Anti-Drug Media Campaign, Spring 2001, p. 5.
5. From the video *Ecstasy*, produced by "In the Mix," the PBS weekly series for teens. Quoted with permission.
6. Substance Abuse and Mental Health Services Administration, National Household Survey on Drug Abuse, Summary Report 1998 (Rockville, MD: Substance Abuse and Mental Health Administration, 1999), p. 13.
7. National Household Survey on Drug Abuse, p. 56.
8. Carey Goldberg, "Needle Trades Pit Science Against Suburb," *The New York Times*, June 23, 2001.

CHAPTER 8

1. www.health.org/reality/whatsnew2000/general/listening.htm
2. www.casacolumbia.org/newsletter_show.htm?doc_id=80623
3. www.casacolumbia.org/newsletter1457/newsletter _show.htm?doc_id=57092
4. Paul A. Winters, editor, *Teen Addiction* (San Diego, CA: Greenhaven Press, 1997), p. 100.
5. www.casacolumbia.org/newsletter1457/newsletter _show.htm?doc_id=57092
6. Annual Report, National Drug Control Strategy (Washington, DC: Office of National Drug Control Policy, 2001), p. 56.
7. Alexandra Marks, "In Drug Treatment vs. Prison, a Political Shift," *Christian Science Monitor*, February 14, 2002.
8. www.casacolumbia.org/newsletter1457/newsletter _show.htm?doc_id=57903
9. www-news.uchiago.edu/releases/96/9609o5.drug. treatment.shtml
10. www.whitehouse.gov/news/releases/2001/05/print/20010510-1.html
11. substanceabuse.about.com/library/bllaw042801.htm
12. "Drug Treatment, Not Prison," *Christian Science Monitor*, July 21, 2000.
13. www.casacolumbia.org/newsletter1457/newsletter _show.htm?doc_id=57093
14. U.S. Department of Health and Human Services, Substance Abuse and Mental Health Services Administration, "Changing

the Conversation: Improving Substance Abuse Treatment"
(Washington, D.C.: SAMSHA, November 2000), pp. 38–39.

15. substanceabuse.about.com/library/bllaw072200.htm
16. Tabitha M. Powledge, "Beating Abuse," *Scientific American*, January 2002, p. 20.
17. www.familywatch.org/library/inwaondr.004.html

CHAPTER 9

1. pbs.org/wgbh/pages/frontline/shows/drugs/buyers/whoare.html
2. www.state.gov/g/inl/rls/nrcpt/2001/rpt/8474.htm
3. Michael Isikoff, "Man Without a Plan," *Newsweek*, September 17, 2001, p. 47.
4. United Nations Office of Drug Control and Crime Prevention, *Economic and Social Consequences of Drug Abuse and Illicit Trafficking* (New York: UNODCCP, 1998), p. 3.
5. www.usdoj.gov/dea/pubs/cngr/test/ct050301.htm
6. Monique Stauder, "Colombian Cocaine Runs Through It," *Christian Science Monitor*, June 13, 2001.
7. Tim Weiner, "With Taliban Gone, Opium Farmers Return to Their Only Cash Crop," *The New York Times*, November 26, 2001.
8. James E. Copple, "Exploring the Explosive and Addictive World of Meth" (Washington, DC: National Crime Prevention Council, CATALYST, April 2001), p. 2.
9. Christopher S. Wren, "A Pipeline of the Poor Smuggles Heroin," *The New York Times*, February 21, 1999.
10. Ellise Pierce, "Underground Railroad," *Newsweek*, March 21, 2001, p. 35.
11. www.dea.gov/pubs/intel/01020/index.html
12. Clifford Krauss, "U.S. Moves to Close Canadian Drug Route for Illegal Stimulants," *The New York Times*, March 3, 2002.
13. drugpolicy.gov/drugfact/
14. www.whitehouse.gov/news/releases/2001/05/print/20010510-1.htm
15. George F. Will, "About Cocaine and Bananas," *Newsweek*, September 17, 2001, p. 78.
16. substanceabuse.about.com/library/weekly/aa100601.htm
17. www.familywatch.org/library/inwaondr.004.html

CHAPTER 10

1. Mike Gray, *Drug Crazy* (New York: Routledge, 2000), p. 190.
2. www.casacolumbia.org/media/drugdecrim.htm

3. www.dare.com/D_ARCH/D_summary_1998_survey.htm
4. "Set It Free," *The Economist*, July 28, 2001, p. 16.
5. www.casacolumbia.org/newseltter_show.htm?doc_id=57093
6. Drug Abuse Update from National Families in Action, October 29, 2001.
7. www.casacolumbia.org/media/drugdecrim.htm
8. Avram Goldstein, *Addiction* (New York: Oxford University Press, 2001), pp. 297–299.
9. www.NORML.org, .Special News Release. October 22, 2001
10. Ted Gottfried, *Should Drugs Be Legalized*? (Brookfield, CT: Twenty-First Century Books, 2000), p. 94.
11. Goldstein, *Addiction*, pp. 282–282.
12. "Marijuana Remains European Illicit Drug of Choice," NORML E-Zine, November 27, 2001.
13. Goldstein, *Addiction*, p. 285.
14. Greg Winter, "U.S. Cracks Down on Medical Marijuana in California," *The New York Times*, October 31, 2001.
15. Quoted in Judge James P. Gray's *Why Our Drug Laws Have Failed and What We Can Do About It* (Philadelphia, PA: Temple University Press, 2001), p. 265.
16. Robert L. DuPont, *The Selfish Brain: Learning from Addiction* (Washington, DC: American Psychiatric Press, 1997), pp. 162–163.

FOR MORE INFORMATION

BOOKS

Courtwright, David E. *Forces of Habit: Drugs and the Making of the Modern World*. Cambridge, MA: Harvard University Press, 2001.

Dowd, Robert. *The Enemy Is Us: How to Defeat Drug Abuse and End the War on Drugs*. Miami, FL: The Hefty Press, 1996.

DuPont, Robert L. *The Selfish Brain: Learning From Addiction*. Minneapolis, MN: Hazelden, 2000.

Friedman, David, and Sue Rusche. *False Messengers: How Addictive Drugs Change the Brain*. The Netherlands: Harwood Academic Publishers, 1999.

Goldstein, Avram. *Addiction: From Biology to Drug Policy*. New York: Oxford University Press, Second Edition 2001.

Gottfried, Ted. *Should Drugs Be Legalized?* Minneapolis: Twenty-First Century Books, 2000.

Hicks, John. *Drug Addiction: No Way I'm an Addict*. Minneapolis: Millbrook Press, 1997.

Hyde, Margaret O., and John F. Setaro, M.D.. *Alcohol 101: An Overview for Teens*. Minneapolis: Twenty-First Century Books, 1999.

Hyde, Margaret O. *Mind Drugs*, 6th ed. Brookfield, CT: Millbrook Press, 1998.

Jay, Jeff, and Debra Erickson Jay. *Love First: A New Approach to Intervention for Alcoholism and Drug Addiction*. Minneapolis, MN: Hazelden, 2000.

Winters, Paul, Editor. *Teen Addiction*. San Diego, CA: Greenhaven Press, 1997.

United Nations Drug Control Programme. *World Drug Report 2000*. New York: United Nations, 2001.

HOT LINES

Cocaine Helpline
800-cocaine (262-2463)
This hot line is operated twenty-four hours a day, seven days a week.

National Drug Information Treatment and Referral Hotline
800-662-HELP (4357)
Spanish-speaking callers: 800-55-AYUDA (2-9832)
This hot line is operated by the National Institute on Drug Abuse and is staffed Monday through Friday 9 A.M. to 3 P.M. and from noon to 3 P.M. on Saturdays and Sundays.

Substance Abuse 24-Hour Helpline and Treatment
1-800-234-0420

E BOOKS AND OTHER HELP

In addition to the information in this book, you can obtain information from many free brochures and news items distributed by the National Clearinghouse for Drug and Alcohol Information (NCADI) at P.O. Box 2345, Rockville, MD 20852, 1-800-788-2800. Or you can access information online at:
www.health.org/multimedia/keywords.asp?Ev..

E books (electronic books) are available from the National Clearinghouse for Alcohol and Drug Information at the address above. These free E books can be used on a PC, laptop, or Pocket PC PDA.

A consortium of more than twenty-five national organizations and networks work to prevent drug abuse in the United States. You can learn more about them by contacting the National Drug Prevention League (NDPL) at www.NDPL.org.

ORGANIZATIONS AND WEB SITES

If you do not have access to a computer, call your public library for further information on the sites given below:

ATLAS (Athletes Training & Learning to Avoid Steroids)
www.atlasprogram.com

The National Center on Addiction and Substance Abuse at Columbia University
www.casacolumbia.org

Centers for Disease Control and Prevention (CDC)
www.cdc.gov

Club Drug Site of National Institute on Drug Abuse (NIDA)
www.clubdrugs.org

Community Anti-Drug Coalitions of America (CADCA)
www.cadca.org

Do It Now Foundation
www.doitnow.org

Monitoring the Future
www.monitoringthefuture.org

National Clearinghouse for Alcohol and Drug Information (NCADI)
www.health.org

National Families in Action (NFIA)
www.nationalfamilies.org

National Household Survey on Drug Abuse
www.health.org/govstudy/bkd376

National Inhalation Prevention Coalition
www.inhalants.org

National Institute on Drug Abuse (NIDA)
www.nida.nih.gov

National Organization for the Reform of Marijuana Laws (NORML)
www.norml.org

National Youth Anti-drug Media Campaign
www.mediacampaign.org

Office of National Drug Control Policy
www.whitehousedrugpolicy.gov

Partnership for a Drug-Free America
www.drugfree.org

Substance Abuse and Mental Health Services Administration (SAMSHA)
www.samhsa.gov

U.S. Drug Enforcement Administration (DEA)
www.dea.gov

White House Office of Drug Policy
www.whitehousedrugpolicy.gov

INDEX